I Wait for You!
Miracles on Main Street

Praise for I Wait for You! Miracles on Main Street

"Whether you are a potential adorer, a seasoned guardian, or a coordinator looking to rejuvenate adoration in your parish, this book will inspire you! It also includes, as an extra gem, valuable tips on growing or beginning adoration in your parish. Our Lord's Presence in the Eucharist is the greatest treasure of our life—the more you consume Him in the Eucharist or are in His Presence in adoration, the more Christlike you become. This book shines with glowing examples of this truth!"

–Bishop Joseph L Coffey
Archdiocese for the Military Services, USA
Vicar for Veterans Affairs

"I identify with the heartfelt accounts of miraculous encounters with our Eucharistic Lord that fill the book *I Wait for You! Miracles on Main Street*. Its blend of testimonies from priests and laity will inspire new adorers and revitalize old ones. The narratives and reflections are masterfully presented."

–Deacon Jim Stahlnecker
Director of "Our Lady of The Eucharist" Perpetual
Eucharistic Adoration Chapel on Staten Island, NY
for over 28 years

"This book is very timely. We are in the midst of the Eucharistic Revival when only 30% of Catholics believe in the True Presence of the Eucharist. This easy-to-read book is a fantastic preparatory tool to use during Eucharistic Adoration so that you can get to *Know Him, Love Him and Serve Him* more and more, and, thereby, grow in holiness. Your mission and mine is eternity with our Lord. Eucharistic Adoration is a taste of *eternity* on earth. Try to bring others with you. What else matters, right?"

–Sr. Deirdre (Sr. Dede) M. Byrne, POSC
Superior, The Little Workers of the Sacred Hearts,
Washington, D.C.

I Wait for You!
Miracles on Main Street

30 Inspirational Accounts from a
Eucharistic Adoration Chapel in a Small
Southern Coastal Town

Missy Treutel Schmidt
and
Kathryn Hayeks White

2023 First Printing

I Wait for You! Miracles on Main Street:
30 Inspirational Accounts from a Eucharistic Adoration
Chapel in a Small Southern Coastal Town

Copyright © 2023 by Missy Treutel Schmidt & Kathryn
Hayeks White

Cover art: © Scott Sumner / Sum Fine Art LLC

Title page art: Kathryn White

ISBN: 979-8-218-27288-3

10 9 8 7 6 5 4 3 2 1

All Scripture verses are from The Catholic Study Bible
(Senior 1990).

Printed in the United States of America

Dedication

This book is lovingly dedicated to the Eucharistic Lord,
present in all the tabernacles
in churches and chapels throughout the world,
with grateful praise.

To Our Lady of Grace, who watched over and guided our
literary adventure, we love you.

To Saint Francis de Sales, patron of authors, your intercession
and timeless words have inspired, directed, and encouraged us
throughout this writing process.

To Kathy Gibbs, our friend and intercessor, may you rest in the
peace of Christ.

Personal Acknowledgments

We want to thank the perpetual adoration guardians and our contributing priests for your generous submissions to this book. You have taken the time to share your heartfelt encounters with Jesus in His Real Presence, and we are deeply grateful.

To all those who have covered us in prayer and support while we wrote this book, especially the Blessed Francis Xavier Seelos Prayer Group at St. Lawrence Catholic Church in Fairhope, Alabama, your prayers have encouraged us and helped us persevere.

To John Martin, we offer our thanks and gratitude for your outstanding editorial review and advice. The wisdom you shared gave us new direction and excitement for this endeavor.

To our amazing technical advisors, Dr. JoAnn Tebbetts, Joanna Almond, and Emily Schmidt, we leaned greatly on your patient generosity, help, and expertise.

We are grateful to Karin Caswell for your tremendous assistance in the book printing process.

We also want to thank Reverend Michael Sreboth, Carter Conger, Judy Nanfito, and Nancy Fontenot for your guidance with this manuscript.

To Tom Hoopes, thank you for sharing the "How to Pray a Holy Hour" resource.

To Deacon Jim Stahlnecker, who spent four to five years calling twenty to thirty chapel coordinators daily to link us together, your diligence has borne great fruit!

We include a special prayer of thanksgiving for our children and grandchildren, our source of inspiration and continual blessings: Chase and Janna, Matthew, Mary Margaret and Chris, Claire and Matthew, Emily, Charlie, Cecilia, Will, Cate, Peter, Fulton and Annie, Michael and April, David, Joanna and David, Connor, Lexi, Lilly, and Will.

Finally, we extend our greatest thanks and gratitude to our two dear husbands, Deacon Ted Schmidt and Larry White. You are our balcony people, always cheering us on in every way. We love you!

To the Reader

To all of you reading *I Wait for You! Miracles on Main Street*, remember that you are reading stories. They are the simple accounts of everyday experiences by people who have encountered the sacramental mystery of the Real Presence of our Lord Jesus Christ in adoration. In their own words they have shared the moments He has touched their hearts and emotions, often in profoundly life-changing ways. With that in mind, please read the following accounts gently and patiently.

In Christ,

Missy Treutel Schmidt

Co-author

In Christ,

Kathryn Hayeks White

Co-author

Contents

Part III Your Miracles Await

Part I
A Chapel is Born

Chapter One

Miracles of Inspiration

Hearing His Voice

*"I will be with you always until the end
of the age." Matthew 28:20*

We Catholics take Him at His Word. Jesus is still physically present with us in every corner of the world. He lovingly waits for us in tabernacles within cathedrals, basilicas, chapels, shrines, and Catholic churches—and now there are more than 800 perpetual adoration chapels in the United States. These "powerhouses of grace" are definitely the Lord's work. Calling us by name, Jesus longs for us to have a share in this amazing grace as we visit Him face to face in Eucharistic Adoration.

What is Eucharistic Adoration? Spiritual writer Philip Kosloski (2017) says, "Eucharistic Adoration is a deeply personal method of prayer that many saints have recommended over the past few centuries. It consists of visiting a church or small chapel to adore Jesus Christ, truly present in the Blessed Sacrament."(Kosloski) Eucharistic Adoration provides the opportunity, while in the silence of a church or chapel, to cultivate an intimate relationship with our Lord, leading to sanctification and holiness. (See Appendix 5 for more information.)

I Wait for You! Miracles on Main Street was inspired by more than a decade of stories shared by weekly Perpetual Eucharistic Adoration guardians—those who keep company with the Lord every hour on the hour around the clock. Originating in our chapel in a small Southern town and its surrounding coastal area, this book is a compilation of inspiring Eucharistic encounters. Each story is as unique and varied as the individuals themselves. Some are bold and breathtaking while others are quietly profound. Woven throughout all the stories is a common thread: Jesus Christ is alive and real, and He is waiting to share His life, miracles, and graces with us in adoration. The manifestation of these glorious fruits from our chapel proves a sublime truth—namely, that perpetual adoration can be, for any parish and its members, a spiritual powerhouse.

God has blessed the Alabama Gulf Coast abundantly. Towering pines, majestic oaks, and a welcoming coastline of sea and sky fill the landscape. The overall rhythm of life is peaceful and friendly. Our parish chapel, Blessed Sacrament Chapel, is located three blocks from Mobile Bay on the Eastern Shore in Daphne, Alabama. Nestled peacefully alongside the main church and within walking distance of the parish school, the chapel receives more than 1000 visitors weekly. During the school year, students from third through eighth grades are eager to make their "Thursday visits" to the Eucharistic Lord.

Lovingly constructed by master craftsman Bill Purvis, our chapel reflects the timeless beauty of coastal architecture. Drawing inspiration from his weekly holy hours (which took place inside the main church's cry room for the first two years of perpetual adoration), Bill sat with our Lord and designed the future chapel to be a place for meditation and peaceful prayer in the presence of the Blessed Sacrament. Its brick exterior and gothic arches replicate the main church as mother and child. Once inside, the tranquil warmth of old heart pine floors, pews, and arches creates an atmosphere for worship. Truly, it is a most fitting home for the Lord.

The purpose of this book is three-fold. The first purpose is to share the story of and steps in forming and maintaining an adoration chapel. Over the years, Missy has been asked by men and women in surrounding parishes and states to help them begin perpetual adoration in their parish. She would tell them it takes prayer, a supportive pastor, and a concentrated effort. In large part, perpetual adoration chapels are lay organized and maintained. Our work is supporting Venerable Fulton Sheen's (2019) prophetic words: "Who is going to save Our Church? It is not our bishops, it is not our priests, and it is not the religious. It is up to you, the people. You have the minds, the eyes, and the ears to save the Church."(Burkepile)

The second purpose of this book is to share the beautiful fruits of our adoration chapel. As the chapel coordinator, Missy has been a first-hand witness of the miracles and graces happening on a regular basis. The guardians themselves began sharing their stories, giving her the nudge to share them with you. As you read, you will gain a glimpse into what committed holy hours yield, transforming the lives of everyday Catholics.

Finally, the third purpose of this book is, if you allow it, to serve as an enhancement to your own prayer before the Blessed Sacrament. Of course, it can be read straight through, but it would be most helpful to use as a source of prayerful meditation during holy hours. Following each encounter is a Scripture passage, a saint's quote, and a reflection to encourage a call to action.

Please pray along with us and see if the Lord is calling you to begin perpetual adoration in your parish. In addition, it is our hope that, as you read the following accounts, you too will hear Jesus calling you to sit a while each week at His side and grow in faith, hope, love, *and an irresistible urge to share with others your own miracles in His Eucharistic Presence.* It seems now is the hour, in the midst of a glorious national Eucharistic Revival, for which the Lord will bless you abundantly!

Our Main Street Miracle

On the cold, wet evening of December 7, 1998, Christ the King's vigil mass for the Feast of the Immaculate Conception was about to begin, and the church parking lots were full. Right next door, the school's gym was teeming with young boys preparing for basketball season. As I slowed to a stop to let my fourth grader out of the car to join his teammates, Matthew was exuberantly telling me about his two starred papers he had received in class earlier that day. He was still looking at me and talking as he crossed in front of my Suburban. In the blink of an eye, a delivery truck came out of nowhere and cleared the slight hill ahead of us, hitting Matthew from behind, throwing him into the air like a rag doll, and then driving over him near the bushes, stopping inches from the church's exterior wall. Frozen in horror, my three-year-old daughter Emily and I watched the whole scene play out before our eyes.

Upon hearing the screech of the truck's tires, many parishioners rushed out of the church to help. I remember hearing prayers hanging in the cold air. The peal of sirens grew louder as the truck driver and several men knelt to bring Matthew up from under the truck. It was then that we discovered the truck had rolled directly over Matthew, its tires miraculously missing him. He had some bruising, but suffered no serious injuries.

Fourteen years later, on that very spot where Matthew had lain, the Blessed Sacrament Chapel was dedicated by

Archbishop Thomas J. Rodi. Truly, it seemed that place had been set aside as holy ground from the beginning.

The start of the Lord's call was significant for me. It came on March 9, 2010, the day my mother died. She had been suffering from the lingering effects of a stroke for more than two years. To care for her, I had stepped out of teaching eighth-grade English and religion at Christ the King Catholic School after nine years. After her death, I thanked the Lord for the grace-filled time I had with her and asked Him to reveal His next plans for me.

In time, my father invited my sister, brother, and me to join him on a Rhine River cruise that he had previously planned to enjoy with my mother. As I was discerning a prompting to start Perpetual Eucharistic Adoration, I prayed to Jesus to reveal His will for me in His Eucharistic Presence during the river cruise through France and Germany.

As we traveled up the Rhine River, I was deeply moved in seeking the Eucharistic Lord in the European cities we visited. My sister Suzy and I made it our mission to find the tabernacle to be with Him a while as we visited some of the Catholic churches, shrines, and cathedrals. Most visits involved searching for the tabernacle tucked away from the tourists. The artifacts and paintings attracted the larger crowds, but Suzy and I knew whom we were seeking, and it was there in those holy moments before Him that the Lord of all ages asked me to begin something new.

Jesus is always leading us; He puts promptings in our hearts. All we need to do is trust in Him and respond. Then He makes it happen.

After receiving an answer to my prayers, the next step was to ask our new pastor, Father Matthew O'Connor, if he would support our lay movement of perpetual adoration.

Our parish was ripe for perpetual adoration. For more than fifteen years, we had supported First Friday 12-hour adoration, which we then increased to 24-hour adoration and finally 36-hour adoration. Now I prayed our pastor would support perpetual adoration.

Father O'Connor's answer was providential. Instead of responding "yes" or "no," he directed me to join a strategic planning meeting scheduled for the next night. The purpose of the meeting was to identify and address the top priorities of our parish. Some of the twenty items on the agenda included church/school building improvements and additions, new school playground equipment, increased campus security and, now, perpetual adoration.

Before the 100-member committee, I passionately shared that, as Catholics, we are the custodians of the Eucharistic Lord—a gift that blesses not only us, but also our entire community. I shared the tremendous benefits perpetual adoration would have on us and our parish families. Finally, I shared that, if we truly trusted that Jesus was alive with us, all our other needs would be met according to His providence.

After each of us presented our needs, the committee members moved into discussion groups to rank the priorities. I remember hoping perpetual adoration would make it into the top five chosen priorities. Imagine my amazement when it was ranked number one!

The next step was to invite a visiting adoration priest to speak at all our masses and our neighboring parishes' masses to gauge interest. After Fr. Victor Warkulwitz finished speaking, he informed us that we would need at least 400 pledges of interest and support to begin perpetual prayer. When all the forms were tallied, we had 757! Continuing to trust in the Lord's providence, I scheduled an informational meeting to recruit Perpetual Eucharistic Adoration committee members. As usual, the Lord, ever faithful, met our every need, and all thirty committee spots were filled.

Finally, we set about making and receiving more than 800 phone calls to fill the 168 weekly hours with two guardians per watch. In the following months, the Lord moved mightily to inspire not only our parishioners, but also parishioners from seven other parishes to claim their holy hours, which ensured perpetual prayer for all. In total, we had committed guardians, consisting of Catholics, Episcopalians, and Anglicans, visiting with Jesus each week, traveling from Daphne, Spanish Fort, Fairhope, Point Clear, Gulf Shores, Mobile, Loxley, Bay Minette, Robertsdale, Foley, and Stockton. When God calls, He provides!

After a full year of preparation, our beloved pastor was pleased with our success. Father O'Connor suggested we begin on Ash Wednesday, and so we did. Christ the King Catholic Church began the powerhouse of perpetual adoration on Ash Wednesday, March 9, 2011—exactly one year from the day of my mother's passing. All glory to the Risen Lord!

For more than twelve years, through hurricane closures, winter freezes, and the COVID shutdown, the Holy Spirit has guided us in steadily maintaining Eucharistic visits. In the first six years, our PEA committee, consisting of twenty-four hourly captains, four division leaders, an invaluable scheduler, and myself, discussed maintenance issues, both physical as well as spiritual. We also discussed new ways of attracting more weekly guardians, meeting every three months.

Some of the more fruitful ways in which we attracted new guardians included weekly guardians giving their personal testimonials after Sunday masses. Their heartfelt stories of productive encounters encouraged new commitments. Additionally, the church bulletin maintained an updated list of hours in need of a second holy hour partner. We also hosted special "boost" speakers to encourage adoration participation. The speakers have included Fathers of Mercy preachers and personal testimony of well- known converts to the Catholic faith.

In our seventh year, our system improved greatly when we moved from pen-and-paper attendance sheets to the implementation of the We Adore Him system, providing iPad hourly sign-in, automated text/email substitute requests, and reminder notifications of scheduled hours. Spanish translations are available when needed. In hindsight, the electronic update was a timely gift from God, which aided us in reopening the chapel quickly after the COVID lockdowns.

How does our chapel function around the clock? Our doors are open to all visitors throughout the day and automatically lock in the evening for security. A key fob entry is required for guardians keeping watch with the Lord from 6 p.m. until 6 a.m. Those wishing to become a night guardian from either Christ the King or a surrounding parish can contact us with a church affiliation, and can be registered after membership verification.

In closing, I am very grateful to share with you the following firsthand encounters of some of our Lord's blessings taking place right here on this holy ground in Daphne, Alabama. As you will discover, just like in the days when Jesus walked the earth as recorded in the Acts of the Apostles, He is still touching, healing and converting us today.

Missy Treutel Schmidt,
Solemnity of Corpus Christi, June 11, 2023

Premonitions

God broke into my life through a moment of unexpected, unforeseen grace. As a young girl, a child of faith, but not of the Catholic faith, my first fleeting experience of the Real Presence of Jesus Christ was in my neighborhood parish church, Blessed Sacrament. Initially, it was the castle-like beauty of the building that captivated me. I never passed by without wondering what treasures it held inside. One day, my curiosity—sufficiently fueled by the allure of the interior—gave me the courage to draw near for a closer look. Climbing the steps to the front porch, I noticed one of the heavy oak doors slightly ajar and, before I knew it, I squeezed the latch, pulled hard, and stepped inside. The quiet stillness of the vestibule embraced me, and I began to explore further. Shafts of sunlight streamed in from windows far above, and my footsteps followed them across the tiled floor toward a second set of doors. For a moment I paused, torn between pursuing and abandoning this daring adventure. Then, quite unexpectedly, a prompting for "more" formed in my ten-year-old heart, and I pushed the sanctuary door wide open, and with that, opened the door to a wonderful spiritual journey.

Once inside the sanctuary, I looked around. The beauty of such a holy place was striking. This church was unlike others I knew. While my gaze roamed the room, my heart responded to the transcendence. Rows of austere wooden pews stood in formation along the center aisle, directing my eyes to the altar. Votive candles by the dozens flickered brightly on either side. Murals above and surrounding the altar depicted familiar Biblical figures, and angels looked down from their celestial home. I knew these people and their stories, and I loved them. My heart lifted, and I drew in a breath of warm, earthy incense. What a place of wonder! Even the ceilings were dressed in patterns of golden finery.

Yet the glorious architecture was not the focus of my attention. My eyes had fastened themselves on the splendid box behind the altar and the red sanctuary candle glowing above. I wouldn't understand their significance until later, but I knew God was here in this place, and in that big, wonderful moment I claimed my treasure. Gazing at the tabernacle in the hush of the darkened sanctuary, God broke through into my life. I stood quietly on the threshold, feeling His touch upon my soul, and I knew He loved me immensely. As a child, I had no words for what I was experiencing; I only knew it quickened a deep desire to know His touch again and again, to know in ever fuller measure the infinite love that summoned me.

I followed that moment of breakthrough all the way into the Catholic faith. Jesus helped me see beyond what is merely visible into what is truly real. The grace I received from the Real Presence of Jesus and the little visits I shared with Him throughout a long and winding spiritual journey nourished and sustained my soul abundantly. Now, so many years later, wonder and gratitude overwhelm me as piercingly as when I was a child standing alone in a darkened sanctuary as I behold love without measure in adoration. It is my prayer that all who read the stories contained within these pages will be drawn, as I was, to our amazing Eucharistic Lord and also experience God breaking through into their lives in many big and small holy moments.

Kathryn Hayeks White

Part II
Fruits Abound

Chapter Two

Miracles of Presence

In the Shadow of Witnesses– Eucharistic Amazement

I write this reflection on these personal encounters of Eucharistic Adoration in the midst of a three-year Eucharistic Revival, declared by the United States Conference of Catholic Bishops on the Feast of Corpus Christi in 2022. The purpose of this revival is to stir up within the faithful Eucharistic amazement. There is a danger, however, in thinking that once we have completed the three-year revival we can move on to something else. But that is precisely what this Eucharistic Revival is intended to address. We can't move on from the Eucharist! The most Blessed Sacrament is, or should be, the center of our lives as Jesus Himself is to be our center and the most Blessed Sacrament is Jesus Himself—Body, Blood, Soul, and Divinity. The Eucharistic Revival, and its Eucharistic amazement, ought to be the disposition of all Catholics at all times.

———— ◇ ————

The Eucharistic Revival, Eucharistic amazement, ought to be the disposition of all Catholics, at all times.

———— ◇ ————

To my delight, all the stories shared by these adorers and weekly guardians demonstrate that they possess this disposition. They understand Eucharistic amazement. Through their commitments and accounts, their lives have been changed as they draw ever closer to the Eucharistic Lord.

They are not alone in their journey. They are following in the shadows of great witnesses before them. For example, St. Dominic, as an itinerant preacher, spent a great deal of time walking from town to town. Although exhausted from his travels, upon entering a town, he immediately went to the Blessed Sacrament to offer praise and thanksgiving to God and to intercede for those to whom he would preach. His time before the Blessed Sacrament rejuvenated him.

Another witness was St. Catherine of Siena, a third-order Dominican like me, who greatly loved Jesus in the Blessed Sacrament. She literally lived only on the Blessed Sacrament for the last seven years of her life. Amazing!

Finally, there was St. John of Cologne, who was martyred in 1572 by non-Catholics after they tortured him and eventually hanged him in the hope he would deny the doctrine of the Eucharist. He never did.

St. Dominic, St. Catherine, and St. John, through your powerful witness, pray for us that we, like all of you, will never lose Eucharistic amazement!

Reverend J. Francis Sofie, Jr., Mobile, AL

❧ 1 ❧ *Devoted to the End*

Kathy Gibbs was a Saturday evening guardian for many years. She was a vivacious woman with a child-like faith and a deep love for Jesus. After two years of suffering, Kathy was diagnosed with stage four stomach cancer. Her decision to stop chemotherapy after only a few treatments, along with her insurance company agreeing to prepay her life insurance, allowed Kathy to spend focused time in her last year with her family and to keep a weekly date with Our Eucharistic Lord in adoration.

Kathy grew up in Bolivia with a devout Catholic upbringing and, when she was eighteen, she married and moved to America. All her life, she had a deep devotion to Jesus and His mother Mary. She radiated love. Kathy's beautiful faith was strengthened by her steadfast devotion to the *15 Prayers of St. Bridget* (Scheenstra n.d.), highlighting the passion of Christ. She shared with me that her mission in this life was to spread the devotion of the *15 Prayers* so people could meditate on what Jesus physically endured for each one of us. When she realized she could spread her devotion through this book, she received total peace. She died less than one hundred days after we spoke. Kathy was forty-one years old.

In loving memory of Kathy, we would like to share the *15 Prayers of St. Bridget* and encourage all to consider praying and meditating on them for one year, as many of us have done in our parish of Christ the King. The ancient prayers give a vivid account of Jesus's sacrifice for all mankind.

Written by Missy Schmidt for Kathy Gibbs, Daphne, AL

Pause and Pray before the Blessed Sacrament—Devoted to the End

"The message of the cross is foolishness to those who are perishing, but to us who are being saved it is the power of God."

1 Corinthians 1:18

"My Lord Jesus Christ, Your blessed, royal, and magnificent heart could never by torments, or blandishments, be swayed from the defense of Your kingdom of truth and justice."

St. Bridget of Sweden (2023)

For Reflection

God reveals His love and power in the message of the cross. Picture Jesus with one arm nailed to the cross and the other arm extended toward you, reaching out, drawing you in close, and holding you in His loving embrace. United on the cross—both He and you, bloody, bruised, and beaten—you find the eternal source of grace and transformation.

What crosses have you suffered for the love of Christ? In the midst of pain, have you been able to unite your suffering to His on the cross and hold on to Him as He is holding on to you? Does the love in your heart reflect the image of the self-sacrificing love of Christ? Look and learn from the cross of Christ, then give thanks for yours.

See Appendix 3 for 15 Prayers of St. Bridget.

2 ∽ *My Eucharistic Home*

In my life, there have been countless encounters with Christ in the Eucharist. Some pass by without much notice, and others are a striking reminder of the great gift that Christ gives us of His Body and Blood in the most Blessed Sacrament.

One such reminder occurred in late August of 2005 as I found myself at St. Joseph's Seminary College following Hurricane Katrina. We were gathered in a candle-lit room waiting for Mass to begin. My heart and mind were consumed by the thought of my home on the Mississippi Gulf Coast. The storm had completely destroyed my physical home and all twelve homes on our family property. Along with destroying my home, it destroyed my sense of home. This land was the place where my great-grandparents were raised and where they decided to raise my grandmother and where she raised my father and where my parents raised me. I had always found peace on this property, and I felt orphaned without this place to call home.

As I reflected on these things, grief filled my heart as the priest began Mass: "In the name of the Father, and of the Son, and of the Holy Spirit." As Mass progressed, familiar phrases such as "this is My Body... this is My Blood... behold the Lamb of God" brought peace. Christ spoke deeply in this celebration and gave me this gift of knowing that the loving peaceful presence of Jesus is always there for us in the Eucharist. My ancestors had found and encountered this same gift of Christ in the Eucharist, and by the time I said "Amen" to the "Body of Christ," I was no longer an orphan, but peacefully at home with a serenity stronger than any storm.

Reverend James N. Morrison, Robertsdale, AL

Pause and Pray before the Blessed Sacrament— My Eucharistic Home

"May the Lord of peace himself give you peace at all times and in every way. The Lord be with you."
2 Thessalonians 3:16

"To visit the Blessed Sacrament is…a proof of gratitude, and expression of love, and a duty of adoration toward Christ the Lord."
Pope Paul VI (CCC, no.1418, Mystery of Faith)

For Reflection

Inner tranquility is found in embracing God's holy will in everything, even those things hard to accept or difficult to understand. Fr. Morrison turned to Mass and found God's peace in the Eucharist, his true steadfast home.

Are you willing to embrace God's holy will in all that happens to you each day? Do you seek His will over and above things you cannot understand or control? Where do you turn to find peace?

❧ *3* ❧ *Angel's Song*

There are angels in His Presence, hovering around our Lord,
Surrounding the Eucharist, all in one accord.

Veiled in mystery and silence, hidden from my sight,
Loving and protecting Him, humbly gazing at me this night.

Where Jesus is the cherubim and seraphim prevail,
Singing songs of thankful praise, before me this unseen veil.

Give me the heart of just one angel that I may look upon His gaze
And sing sweetly to Him a prayerful song of praise.

Warm tears swell my eyes as more real His Presence becomes,
Glimpsing His blood-veined body, the more I see the less I become.

Tender is His mercy; loving is His care.
Wrapped in silence this night, my moments with Him so rare.

Mary Francis, Daphne, AL

Pause and Pray before the Blessed Sacrament— Angel's Song

"I am the Bread of Life." *John 6:48*

"The soul of one who loves God always swims in joy, always keeps holiday, and is always in the mood for singing."
St. John of the Cross (De Sola Chervin 2003, 175)

For Reflection

As the Eucharistic Prayer begins, the priest says, "Lift up your hearts." The veil between heaven and earth is opened, and we are lifted up to join with myriads of angels and every creature to worship God in one accord. *Angel's Song* captures the glorious spiritual reality of the angel's constant vigil before our Lord in the monstrance.

While you are in adoration, ask for "the heart of just one angel," and sing Him a "prayerful song of praise."

❧ 4 ☙ Re-Creation

I love my Catholic faith, everything about it. I especially love when, at the consecration, the priest prays over the bread and wine, and the miracle of transubstantiation happens. I love the whole mystical, heavenly reality of Jesus being hidden in the Blessed Sacrament. It is the miracle of the Eucharist that drew me, a convert, into the church years ago, but it is in the many hours of Eucharistic Adoration where the miracle plays out in my life.

As a new Catholic, I remember my first steps into Catholicism being tentative. The reality of how small I was in the shadow of such a vast church loomed over me, and I was unsure if I would be able to successfully navigate its immense and ancient corridors. Embracing my new faith fully, I went exploring along the highways

> I have learned the silence of the chapel is a place of sanctification.

and byways of Catholicism, unaware that Jesus was so close outside of Mass. Imagine my delight when I discovered He, a real living person, was waiting for me in the adoration chapel!

I have learned the silence of the chapel is a place of sanctification, and in His Eucharistic Presence I receive the transformative power and miracle of the sacrament. The God of heaven opens my heart and mind and pours Himself into me so that little by little, hour by hour, the "old" me diminishes and the "new" me is taking its place.

I am not the same person I once was. Gazing upon Jesus in the monstrance is giving me new wings on which to soar. He is re-creating me.

When I contemplate the immeasurable generosity of God for this gift, I want my entire life to prove my gratitude. Growing, changing, living, learning, breathing in God in adoration, then exhaling His spirit on the world after I leave is, for me, the miracle of sweet salvation.

Kathryn Hayeks White, Daphne, AL

Pause and Pray before the Blessed Sacrament— Re-Creation

"All of us, gazing with unveiled face on the glory of the Lord, are being transformed into the same image from glory to glory, as from the Lord who is the Spirit."

2 Corinthians 3:18

"When I entered the chapel, once again the majesty of God overwhelmed me. I felt that I was immersed in God, totally immersed in Him and penetrated in Him, being aware of how much the heavenly Father loves us. (491)"

St. Faustina Kowalska (2003, 213)

For Reflection

Interior transformation takes place on a day-to-day basis through prayer and meditation. The wonderful effect of a constant union with God is that, in a sense, your daily life of Christ-likeness releases into the world channels of grace for people in need.

While you are before the Lord in adoration, give thanks that He is doing the holy work of transformation within you and pray your daily life may become a source and channel of actual grace for others.

❧ 5 ❧ *The Colors of Love*

It is two o'clock in the afternoon. I walk into the vestibule of St. Lawrence Catholic Church. The darkened church is an invitation from God to come inside and rest in Him. The walls of the church become a fortress blocking out the noise and distractions of the outside world. A point of bright white light draws me close, its simplicity more riveting than anything else in the church. I bow down before You in the host on my knees. I surrender my nothingness. I sit gazing at Your face, Jesus. The peaceful silence envelops me. I close my eyes. The sounds of *O Salutaris Hostia* from the morning Benediction echo in my head. The scent of incense is still in the air. I listen to the intake of my breath and the beating of my heart; they are the only measure of time. My eyes open. A rainbow of color is streaming over the sanctuary from the southern stained-glass window. I feel the Presence of the Spirit allowing them to dance on the north wall. I focus on the largest area of color, the red of the sacred heart of Jesus. The blue of Mary surrounds it on either side. Yellows, greens, and purples move around them both like angels and saints. I watch them as they flicker and slowly fade. I am aware that each moment is here and gone. I look back to Your face in the host. You are here with me. It is now close to three o'clock; the hour of Your death is the hour of greatest mercy. Jesus, I trust in You. I lift my eyes to Your figure on the cross. My sins nailed You to that cross. You redeemed my life with Your own life. How can I repay You for all the good You have done for me? It is 3:08.

I kneel lower before You in the host as I leave. I know I am nothing without You. Your sacrifice has allowed me to become a child of Your father. I am content.

Ruth M. Donelan, Fairhope, AL

Pause and Pray before the Blessed Sacrament— The Colors of Love

"And the Word became flesh and made His dwelling among us."

John 1:14

"Godhead here in hiding, whom I do adore. Masked by these bare shadows, shape, and nothing more. See, Lord, at thy service low lies here a heart, lost all in wonder at the God thou art."

St. Thomas Aquinas (Pitre 2015, 23)

For Reflection

With warmth and understanding, the title *The Colors of Love* acknowledges that our Lord is fully present, dwelling among us in Eucharistic Adoration. The mingling of heaven and earth, of body and spirit, produces a wonder and goodness beyond words. This shows us that, in and through the love and light of God, we are able to contemplate our lives in Him.

The next time you are in adoration, look around and take it all in; with all your senses experience the transcendent God. Then, pray in humble worship for all His goodness surrounding you.

❧ *6* ❧ *He Looks at Me*

The greatest of all parish priests is also our patron, St. John Vianney. For many, many years he was a pastor of a little town in southern France named Ars. He knew the people by name, and they knew him.

One of his parishioners, a farmer named Jacques, was in the habit of coming into the church very early in the morning and spending an hour in quiet with Jesus in the Blessed Sacrament. Every morning he knelt there and sat very quietly, just looking at the tabernacle.

One day after his holy hour, Father Vianney said to him: "Jacques, every day I see you come here at the same hour and spend time with our Lord. I noticed you don't say anything, and you don't use any prayer books. Tell me, what is your experience of Jesus when you come to our church?"

—— ◇ ——

Adoration of the Blessed Sacrament is a foretaste of heaven.

—— ◇ ——

He responded, "Father, it's wonderful. He looks at me, and I look at Him!"

That is the essence of adoration of the Blessed Sacrament. We allow Jesus to look at us, His disciples, and we have the chance to look at Him, our Lord. In this way, adoration of the Blessed Sacrament is a foretaste of heaven when, by the mercy of God, we will see Jesus face-to-face and enjoy His Presence forever.

Very Reverend Paul Zoghby, Foley, AL

Pause and Pray before the Blessed Sacrament— He Looks at Me

"My soul rests in God alone, from whom comes my salvation. God alone is my rock and salvation, my fortress; I shall never fall."

Psalm 62:1–2

"For the greatest things are accomplished in silence— not in the clamor and display of superficial eventfulness, but in the deep clarity of inner vision; in the almost imperceptible start of decision, in quiet overcoming and hidden sacrifice."

Fr. Romano Guardini (1937)

For Reflection

The spiritual gifts of time spent in a church or chapel are immeasurable. The soul who sits in the presence of Jesus, the Lamb of God, the Lord of Peace, the Word of Life, becomes more beautiful in every way. He truly waits to renew and transform you.

Make a greater effort to draw closer to Jesus in the Blessed Sacrament. Resolve to make a visit to Him in the coming week.

Chapter Three

Miracles of Encounter

☙ 7 ☙ *The Eucharist Makes the Priest*

A pivotal moment in my journey to the priesthood happened during a morning mass at St. Pius X in Mobile, Alabama. Fr. Matthew O'Connor had just elevated the sacred host and said those penetrating words: "This is my Body." Peace and confidence radiated from him when he beheld our Lord, and the thought entered my mind for the first time that this work—God's work of proclaiming the Kingdom of Heaven—was something I could do. That evening, the call, unaddressed since my teenage years, became a conscious reality to me. I clearly understood the priesthood was the life He wanted me to lead and, filled with emotion, I cried profusely that night.

Journeying as a priest for fifteen years now, I have learned that the quiet peace of Eucharistic Adoration before weekday masses are the best hours of my week. There I see the Lord, and He sees me. The silence of the small, dimly lit chapel amplifies the richness He offers in the divine life, and I draw deeply from the well of His love. With His grace to fortify me and His Eucharistic Presence to accompany me, I am fully equipped to sojourn on in the shepherding role of Christ. Every need and circumstance I have is shared with Him as we converse and—should there be a storm in my heart—He is there to calm the tumultuous sea and bring my soul home to safe harbor.

Christ has shown me that consistent encounter with the Holy Eucharist cannot but help smooth the rough edges of one's character, give one hope, and—dare it be said—provide one with real joy in this journey through life, for He alone is the only food that can satisfy the hunger of a world starving for real love.

Reverend Stephen Hellman, Monroeville, AL

Pause and Pray before the Blessed Sacrament— *The Eucharist Makes the Priest*

"For my eyes have seen your salvation."

Luke 2:30–31

"We ourselves, with our whole being, must be adoration and sacrifice, and by transforming our world, give it back to God. The role of the priesthood is to consecrate the world so that it may become a living host, a liturgy."

Pope Benedict XVI (Becklo 2022, 83)

For Reflection

As Fr. Hellman moved toward a deeper encounter with the Holy Eucharist, he allowed Jesus to smooth his rough edges. God provides the means for spiritual victory through humility and trust. By growing in the virtues of faith, hope, and charity, peace and joy follow as a natural consequence.

Spend time with our Lord in humble adoration and ask Him to help you recognize your rough edges and allow Him to transform you more into His image.

∽ *8* ∽ *But Wait, There's More!*

After fifty-eight mostly joyful and lively years shared with my husband and children, who wanted to know and embrace the whole world, expanding and accepting more has readjusted my introverted personality. A retreat weekend encouraged me to deepen my spiritual life and, after my husband's death, I decided an adoration hour was exactly what I needed. My desire was for private, treasured time alone, just Jesus and me, so I became a guardian of the ten o'clock evening hour at the chapel. During these treasured hours, I witnessed the Body of Christ, the Church, as more than my perspective of just "Jesus and me." Week by week I grew to know and love the sprinkling of souls who came to the chapel before and after my hour. We were all different in personality and gifts, yet each week we came, bringing our own beauty and diversity to worship and adore as Church, members of one body. Connecting with them even briefly at the chapel, I witnessed the importance of companions on our faith journeys.

But wait, there's more! Now when I arrive at the chapel just before ten o'clock, I am welcomed by thirty seconds of air hugs from the departing guardians and prayer warriors, and we exchange silent assurances of each other's good wishes and prayers.

But wait, there's more! My adoration partner and I have developed a special bond through our shared presence with our Lord. We quietly converse with each other for a few moments while walking back to our cars at eleven o'clock after our adoration hour. I have grown to love this young woman and count it a gift and blessing to know her.

But wait, there's more! My daughter and son-in-law decided they need to drive "Mumsie" to the chapel at such a late hour, and now their presence with me is pure joy and a peaceful end to the day. So, you see it really isn't just "Jesus and me." The beautiful revelation of more for this introvert was learning though we may come to the chapel seeking Jesus in different ways and for different needs, yet we all come for *one* purpose: to adore His Eucharistic Presence as the Church, the Body of Christ.

Pat D'Olive, Fairhope, AL

Pause and Pray before the Blessed Sacrament— But Wait, There's More!

"The cup of blessing that we bless, is it not a sharing in the Blood of Christ? The bread that we break, is it not a sharing in the Body of Christ? Because there is one bread, we who are many are one body, for we all partake of the one bread."

1 Corinthians 10:16–17

"Love everyone with a deep love based on charity...here I do not refer to the simple love of charity we must have for all men but of the spiritual friendship by which two, three, or more souls share with one another their devotion and spiritual affections and establish a single spirit among themselves. Such fortunate souls may justly sing, Behold how good and pleasant it is for brothers to dwell together in unity."

St. Francis de Sales (Ryan 1972, 174–5)

For Reflection

The Catechism of the Catholic Church states, "Through the Eucharist Christ unites the faithful in one body—the Church" (United States Catholic Conference 2007, 1396). The Eucharist is the bread of brotherhood, making us one. It is our job to radiate the love of Christ to our environments and bring about widespread positive outcomes in our personal life as well as in the lives of others.

When you are before Jesus in Eucharistic Adoration, ask Him how you can better radiate the love of Christ more fully in your environments.

❧ 9 ❧ *Tabernacle*

One afternoon I walked into St. Lawrence Catholic Church, genuflected, and sat down in the front pew to spend a few moments with Jesus. On a sunny afternoon, St. Lawrence Catholic Church is a wonderful stop. The lights are off, and sunlight streams in through windows from above. During this afternoon's stop, I sat quietly, contemplating the beauty of the scene: the sunlight, the altar, and the smell of candles and incense, all while knowing our Lord was present.

A carpenter by trade, I was admiring the craftsmanship of the tabernacle when a question formed in my mind: "Lord, why do some people physically suffer more than others?" I have learned when I ask such specific questions not to expect a voice to talk directly to me. I know God will always answer my prayers with "yes," "not now," or "I have something better planned for you." This in itself is a great comfort.

My question on that day was sparked not out of despair, but out of curiosity as both of my sons deal with serious, chronic health issues on a daily basis. I sat a while longer, staring at the tabernacle, thinking that the prayers being offered for my sons were for a healing of their bodies, their physical earthly tabernacles that will ultimately fail. Then my thoughts elevated.

Prayer extends so much farther. It reaches what dwells *inside* our tabernacles—that is, our souls. Just as Jesus dwells inside the tabernacle on the altar, the Holy Spirit dwells with the souls of my sons inside their earthly tabernacles. Prayers offered for healing become prayers for salvation. Wow! In union with the sufferings of Christ, healing prayers extend to both their body *and* souls, effectively making them co-redeemers with Christ.

I left the church, got in my truck, and started the engine. The radio was on and tuned to our local Catholic station. The first words I heard were from Fr. Larry Richards hammering home what had just been revealed to me about our earthly tabernacles. He said, "When we go into a Catholic church, we genuflect in the direction of the tabernacle. We aren't genuflecting to the box, no matter how beautiful it is, but to our Lord who dwells within. He is the object of our prayer and adoration. When we are baptized, we receive the Holy Spirit. Our physical bodies become the tabernacle where the Holy Spirit dwells."

Since this experience, I have found myself looking for Christ in everyone's tabernacles, and I thank the Lord for illuminating the mystery and miracle of redemptive suffering to me.

Larry White, Daphne, AL

Pause and Pray before the Blessed Sacrament— *Tabernacle*

"Now I rejoice in my sufferings for your sake, and in my flesh, I am filling up what is lacking in the afflictions of Christ on behalf of his body, which is the church."

Colossians 1:24

"It is not so much what people suffer that makes the world mysterious, it is how much they miss when they suffer...Why then cannot pain be made redemption? Why cannot we use a cross to become God-like? There is only one way we can become like Him, and that is in the way He bore His sorrows and His Cross. And that way was with love. It is love that makes pain bearable."

Archbishop Fulton Sheen (1990)

For Reflection

Everyone suffers at some point, and most people love someone who suffers. Understanding as well as practicing redemptive suffering is one of the greatest gifts we can give others and the world.

Reflect on a time when you have stood at the foot of the cross for someone. Has there been a time when you were on the cross and someone was there for you? Spend some time before Jesus contemplating the meaning of "in my flesh I am filling up what is lacking in the afflictions of Christ."

❧ *10* ❧ *It's My Mother*

My forty-two-year-old goddaughter was injured in a serious auto accident and lived for five years afterwards in great pain and difficulty. When she passed away, I asked Jesus, "Why didn't you show us how to live with the brokenness we have suffered following my niece's horrible injury?" Grief swept over me, and I wept bitterly.

Five years after her death, a "still small voice" came to me with words of great comfort as I prayed in the adoration chapel. "It's my mother," spoke the voice. Again, I wept, only this time tears of gratitude.

Our Mother Mary does show us how to live through painful tragedy. Hers was to witness Jesus's crucifixion and death. Her pain and sorrow lasted her lifetime. She meets us in Jesus's Presence in the sacraments, especially in the Eucharist and in the holy hours of adoration of her Son in the Blessed Sacrament.

The Holy Spirit's graces are continually at work to dispel debilitating grief and help us trust God's plan. Grace helps us wait for God to work all things for our good and for His great glory.

Judy Sullivan, Spanish Fort, AL

Pause and Pray before the Blessed Sacrament— It's My Mother

"The Mighty One has done great things for me, and holy is His name."

Luke 1:49

"In the Mass and in Eucharistic Adoration we meet the merciful love of God that passes through the Heart of Jesus Christ."

John Paul II (1999)

For Reflection

John Paul II said, "The supernatural virtue of hope gives vision to the mind, strength to the will, courage to the heart, and endurance to the body. It brings a sense of security to the soul." The rosary prayers conclude by directing our hearts toward hope: *Turn then, most gracious advocate, thine eyes of mercy towards us, and after this our exile, show unto us the blessed fruit of your womb, Jesus.*

Resolve today to work to place your disappointments, pain, and sorrows in the heart of Jesus and His loving mother. Then, offer a Hail Mary for hope—the very sweetness of our life.

❧ 11 ❧ *Prayer of Quiet*

What a priceless gift adoration is for me! I believe with all my heart that the many, many special hours spent adoring my Lord and God in the Blessed Sacrament are efficacious, blessing the lives of others. I just cannot imagine my life without weekly time spent with Jesus, praying, listening, singing (only when alone with Jesus in the chapel), and—oh, yes—here and there, falling asleep with my Lord!

My holy hour has been after midnight for many years, and though I strongly resist the temptation to slumber, now and then it happens during those early morning hours. Remembering the words of our Lord to His apostles in the garden, "Stay here and keep watch with me…watch and pray" *(Matthew 26:38)*, left me feeling as though I were failing Jesus by not being able to watch with Him for one hour, even after trying my best to stay awake. What brought consolation was when I learned that well-known saints also experienced drowsiness during adoration or prayer time, just like me. One of those, St. Francis de Sales, gave sage counsel with these words:

> This is the best way of remaining in God's Presence: to will to be forever a source of God's pleasure. Even in our deepest sleep we are in God's Presence, and on awakening we know we have not been absent or separated from Him…. In this prayer of quiet, the will seeks God's good pleasure. The soul wants only to be in God's sight and to please him. The prayer of quiet is excellent, having no mixture of self-interest…

to be content in God's will, not our own.

(de Sales, Francis, 1994)

I still must resist slumber, but with this new understanding, now I thank Jesus for the gift of perfect rest within His will. My whole being is open to His calling without the distractions that come when I am awake. Now my response to Him is: "Speak, Lord, your servant is listening." Jesus, I trust in You!

Beth Perkins, Mobile, AL

Pause and Pray before the Blessed Sacrament— Prayer of Quiet

"Speak Lord, for your servant is listening."

1 Samuel 3:10

"I should be distressed that I drop off to sleep during my prayers...but I don't feel at all distressed. I know that children are just as dear to their parents whether they are asleep or awake. So, I just think that God knows our frame; he remembers that we are dust."

St. Therese of Lisieux (The Catholic Storeroom n.d.)

For Reflection

God sees our humanness. To be so comfortable in closeness and intimacy with Him that we occasionally slumber denotes total entrustment. We become like sleeping children in His arms, remaining always in His Presence yet not knowing it.

Resisting slumber during prayer may be a challenge. The next time you struggle, instead of feeling guilty, pause for a moment to reflect: perhaps this is a time when you have settled into His arms, have said what is in your heart, have attempted to listen, and then, in the comfort of His love, you can now fall asleep.

❧ *12* ❧ *Adoration and Assisi*

Those who know me know my love for Italy in general and for Assisi in particular. Could I live there? Yes, I could, and yes, I have (at least for a month of sabbatical seven years ago). What draws me? The palpable spirit of St. Francis is, of course, a major attraction for me. All the holy places are special: the Basilica, where he is buried in the crypt; the Porziuncola, where he died; Santa Chiara, the burial place of his first female follower and the current home of the San Damiano Crucifix; and San Damiano itself, where Francis first perceived the call to a life of penance and joyful witness.

When I am in Assisi, even if for only a couple of nights, I spend at least one evening at San Damiano. From the center of the town (Piazza del Commune), it's about a mile and a half to the church (now expanded from the times when Francis set about rebuilding it). I walk past Santa Chiara, through a city gate, and down through a park to a parking area. From there, I cross a relatively major street and keep walking down a footpath to the church. Yes, it is all downhill, making the trip back to Assisi special! And it is also dark; it is not dangerous due to a fear of robbers, but traffic.

I always make this trek. Why? The answer is simple. I find tremendous peace when the friars gather for evening prayer and adoration. The music is simple, the liturgy is peaceful, and the adoration is so comforting and contemplative! Others agree, especially in the "high season," which requires arriving at least a half an hour in advance to get a seat. Often the back doors of the chapel are opened up, with chairs in the courtyard, for the regular overflow of folks who want to worship and feel strength in the Eucharistic Presence. The walk back uphill is strenuous (I am not getting any younger), but I am always invigorated with peace and prayer afterward.

Do I need to go to Assisi to find peace and prayer? No. My parish, Our Savior Catholic Church, radiates the same peace, with Eucharistic exposition all day on Wednesdays and on First Friday mornings. And, yes, I feel that strength then, too, but Assisi claims me, and Eucharistic Adoration is a big reason why.

Reverend David Tokarz, Mobile, AL

Pause and Pray before the Blessed Sacrament— Adoration and Assisi

"Peace I leave with you; my peace I give to you. Not as the world gives do I give it to you. Do not let your hearts be troubled or afraid."

John 14:27

"Out of the darkness of my life, so much frustrated, I put before you the one great thing to love on earth: the Blessed Sacrament.... There you will find romance, glory, honor, fidelity, and the true way of all your loves upon earth..."

J. R. R. Tolkien (Carpenter 2012, 53–4)

For Reflection

Read *John 6*: "The Eucharist is the source and summit of our Catholic faith." Evening prayer and Eucharistic Adoration in the chapel at San Damiano "claimed" Fr. Tokarz. Greater still, the "one great thing to love on earth: the Blessed Sacrament" (Carpenter 2012, 53) is always near us and there for the claiming in our Catholic churches and chapels.

Does your life reflect this central belief about the Eucharist? Make it a priority to seek and adore Jesus wherever you should roam on your next vacation.

Chapter Four

Miracles of Discernment

❧ 13 ❧ *A School for Danielle*

When our daughter Danielle was entering eighth grade, I began praying almost every morning at the adoration chapel, asking for discernment as to which Catholic high school she would be attending the next school year. It was a difficult decision for our family as St. Michael in Fairhope, AL, was close to home, but McGill-Toolen in Mobile, AL, was my alma mater. Danielle really wanted to cheer for the McGill-Toolen squad, but she was suffering a congenital foot condition that might possibly require surgery. She had been in and out of a boot for weeks at a time over the last few years, and she felt fortunate to be able to cheer her eighth-grade year despite all the problems.

Continuing to pray for guidance in the matter, one morning while leaving the chapel, I met Fr. Victor Ingalls and asked him his thoughts. He was very kind and said, "The best thing you can do is exactly what you are doing: Place your concerns at the feet of the Lord every day. God will guide you. Trust in that prayer."

In the meantime, Danielle was vacillating between the two schools. In the spring, several girls tried out for the McGill-Toolen squad and, despite her foot pain, Danielle prepared, worked hard, and made the squad. She was excited at the possibility of attending school there; however, St. Michael remained a contender. Imagine our delight when a few days later we received a letter from McGill-Toolen that she had received a scholarship! I'll never forget dropping to my knees and thanking God for the sign we needed to continue with her high school journey!

Danielle went on to enjoy four years of high school, participated on the cheer squad, and received a wonderful Catholic education at my alma mater. The power of prayer has always existed in my life, but this answer was one of the best and unique close moments I have ever experienced.

Maria Payne, Daphne, AL

Pause and Pray before the Blessed Sacrament— A School for Danielle

"Live as children of the light, for light produces every kind of goodness, and righteousness and truth. Try to learn what is pleasing to the Lord."

Ephesians 5:8b–10

"My sweetest joy is to be in the presence of Jesus in the Holy Sacrament. I beg that when obliged to withdraw in body, I may leave my heart before the Holy Sacrament. How I would miss Our Lord if He were to be away from me by His essence in the Blessed Sacrament!"

St. Katharine Drexel (August 2022)

For Reflection

Constant prayer for discernment leads us into the Lord's will. If we are open to His promptings, Jesus can give us a fresh perspective, enabling us to see what He sees. As our trust in the Lord grows, we become a beacon of light for others.

Give the Lord your deepest concern today. Let Him give you His peace in return.

೪14೦ *Lifting the Veil*

It was really very simple: I had to discern whether God was asking me to quit my job. For about two months, this was my prayer at the adoration chapel.

For years I had performed ultrasounds for an infertility doctor. It seemed like the perfect job. I was able to be with my children, keep my ultrasound skills up to date, and be an almost full-time mom. I had prayed for this job for many years and, when it fell into my lap, I thought it was an answer to my prayer.

Once I started listening to Catholic radio, I began to realize how poorly I had been catechized. As I listened, learned, and grew in my faith, an unsettled feeling spread over my soul, disturbing my peace. Doubts about working in this position began to dominate my thoughts, and I became increasingly aware that my conscience was prompting me to discern whether I should stay or leave a job that had at one time seemed ideal.

For two months I spent time in prayer during my adoration hours, asking God if quitting my job was what He wanted me to do, and He gave me clear affirmation day after day. I heard His answer as: "Yes, Debbie, I'm asking you to quit your job." Still, multiple times a day, I would offer up the same petition, and His answer never wavered; it was crystal clear.

Throughout this time of discernment, He allowed a cloudy veil to be lifted from my mind, and when clarity came, it left me with a feeling of indescribable love and a supernatural peace. I believe He let me feel this wonderful peace to reassure me of any lingering doubts in my mind. I didn't want this tangible love to leave, although I knew it would, and eventually the veil lowered again. Yet having opened myself to the wisdom and strength of the Holy Spirit, I understood God's will and submitted my resignation. His beautiful Presence was near me then and for several days afterward in a powerful way.

Debbie Jones, Daphne, AL

Pause and Pray before the Blessed Sacrament—Lifting the Veil

"Trust in the Lord with all your heart, on your own intelligence do not rely. In all your ways be mindful of Him and He will make straight your paths."

Proverbs 3:5,6

"God guides all by the action of His grace. Therefore, do not be lazy or lose heart, but call to God day and night to entreat Him to send you help from above to teach you what to do."

St. Anthony the Great (De Sola Chervin 2003, 211–2)

For Reflection

Silence is vital to spiritual growth. It is where we hear God speaking to us, helping us to discern His will. Spending time in silence helps develop clarity about every aspect of our lives and brings peace to our souls. Debbie sought out the quiet of the chapel and listened for God to speak His will for her life.

In the presence of the Blessed Sacrament, setting aside your desires, when have you last asked God, "What do *You* think I should do?"

∾*15*∾ *Promptings*

I was blessed to serve as the parochial vicar at Christ the King Church in Daphne, AL, for two years. During my time there, I experienced *many* grace-filled moments in the perpetual adoration chapel. It was there that Christ spoke, consoled, and inspired me and many others.

During my second year there, the youth minister of seventeen years announced that her family was moving, so she would no longer be able to serve the parish. Jamie had built an incredible program, and it was hard to imagine anyone being able to step into her shoes to sustain the program as well as continue to cultivate the life of the Holy Spirit moving amongst the teens.

The entire parish, including Father Matthew O'Connor and myself, began the search for a new youth minister. Early in the process, we received an application from Kristen, a Spring Hill College graduate. Kristen had already developed connections with different ministries in the area, including as a semester assistant to Jamie at Christ the King—a seemingly perfect fit for the opening! I gave thanks to God for answering our prayer so quickly and felt a sense of relief about the future of the youth ministry. Unfortunately, a couple of weeks later, Kristen withdrew her application, and we were back to square one.

A short time passed, and the looming vacancy was bearing down on me. I sought the Lord in the adoration chapel one day to be in His Presence and to ask His guidance. As I sat with Jesus, I relayed to Him our situation and asked what we should do. After some time in prayer, I was surprised as I felt Him nudge me to call Kristen. I reminded Him that she was no longer available, yet He kept insisting that I call Kristen.

I then explained to Him how awkward it would be for me to call somebody to gauge their interest in a job they had already clearly decided against. Again, I kept feeling Christ say, "Call Kristen."

Mustering up some faith, I prayed, left the chapel, and called her. On what seemed like the last ring, she answered, and we had an extended conversation. She shared that the timing of my call was more than a coincidence. She had been feeling that, due to circumstances at her current job, the Lord was prompting her to make changes in her life.

Shortly after this conversation, she was hired as our new youth minister. I marveled as I got to know her and watched her move confidently into the role. She served the teens beautifully for five years, advancing the ministry in a way only she could have. Her servant heart and steadfast spirit were an inspiration for the young people growing in their faith. She even helped some to answer calls to the seminary and religious life.

I thank Jesus for His inspiration that day in the chapel and for making it clear to Kristen He was calling her to Daphne. This experience, among others, deepened my trust in Him with all the details of my life and ministry. I pray it will encourage others to do the same.

Reverend Victor P. Ingalls, Mobile, AL

Pause and Pray before the Blessed Sacrament—Promptings

"But the Lord was not in the wind; after the wind and earthquake—but the Lord was not in the earthquake; after the earthquake, fire—but the Lord was not in the fire; after the fire, a small still voice."

1 Kings 19:11,12

"God speaks in the silence of the heart; listening is the beginning of prayer."

St. Teresa of Kolkata (Stephen 2021)

For Reflection

Promptings are real. God uses His "still small voice" as a passage for the Holy Spirit to enter the experiences of our everyday lives—and for good reason. However, these gentle promptings are just that: gentle promptings. God has given us the free will to choose to respond or not. Fr. Victor moved in obedience to the "nudges" he was receiving, and look how God blessed his obedience!

While you are before the Blessed Sacrament, are you listening for His "still small voice" in those little promptings, inspirations, or thoughts embracing your soul? Look, listen, and learn how He makes His will known in obedience!

Chapter Five

Miracles of Healing

༄ 16 ༄ *A Timely Invitation*

I go where I am invited. I was not enrolled in the Rite of Christian Initiation for Adults (RCIA), but was invited by a friend to attend with him one night at Christ the King Catholic Church in Daphne, AL. On this particular evening, the class was discussing with passion the power of Eucharistic Adoration to change lives. We were then invited to go across the street and visit Jesus in the adoration chapel, so I went. When I entered, I was unsure of how to show proper reverence to Him, so I bowed before the Blessed Sacrament and knelt in prayer. At the time, I had no specific needs or prayers in mind; I was simply in a peaceful, open stillness.

Suddenly, in a burst of thought, I saw my mother broken, my father broken, my brother broken, and myself broken. For the previous six years, my brother had been living in California, estranged from the family after an argument

——— ◇ ———

He responded gently, "Bring them here."

——— ◇ ———

that had torn our family apart. Distressed and in tears, I asked the Lord, "What would you have me do?"

He responded gently, "Bring them here."

The intensity of the anger between my brother and parents and the fact that we were not Catholic made this seemingly simple request a challenge requiring supernatural help. With faith, I approached my parents first. Although they were taken aback by what I was asking, they eventually agreed to meet with their estranged son in the chapel. Encouraged by their response, I reached out to my brother. We had not spoken in six years, and I did not expect him to return my call. To my surprise, he called me back within an hour, and I straightaway invited him to come to Alabama to the adoration chapel as a family with us, and he agreed!

Unfortunately, COVID hit, and our plans were delayed. We have yet to visit the chapel together, but the steps Christ helped us take toward reconciliation have been fruitful. Since I reached out to them, my brother phones our parents regularly; apologies have been made, and we are no longer broken, but reconciled.

Since this transformative encounter in the chapel, I enrolled in RCIA and have been received into the Church. I now extend the same timely invitation of Christ that I received to others: Come to the chapel and experience Him, the true source and summit of meaning, purpose, and life.

Jeffrey, Daphne, AL

Pause and Pray before the Blessed Sacrament— A Timely Invitation

"Put on then, as God's chosen ones, holy and beloved, heartfelt kindness, humility and gentleness, and patience, bearing with one another and forgiving one another; as the Lord has forgiven you, so must you also do."

Colossians 3:12, 13

"Grace has five effects in us: first, our soul is healed; second, we will good; third, we work effectively for it; fourth, we persevere; fifth, we break through to glory."

St. Thomas Aquinas (De Sola Chervin 2003, 94)

For Reflection

The Catechism says: "In refusing to forgive our brothers and sisters, our hearts are closed, and their hardness makes them impervious to the Father's merciful love; but, in confessing our sins, our hearts are opened to His Grace" (United States Catholic Conference 2007, 2839–2840).

Reflect upon a time when someone forgave you or you forgave someone. How did that impact your relationship? Today, resolve to be forgiven, and forgive another.

❧ *17* ❧ *A Sign of Hope*

When I received the devastating news that the biopsy revealed I had stage four pancreatic cancer, many anxious thoughts filled my mind. Yet through it all, I clearly heard the words *"Ecce ancilla Domine...*behold, I am the handmaid of the Lord, let it be done unto me according to Thy Word." The words of Our Lady resounded in many of the books I had been reading, and I understood God had been preparing me for the greatest battle of my life. The hourly commitment at the adoration chapel was where I gained courage, found solace, and explored the perfect reading material to strengthen me as I pushed forward. It felt almost as if I had a librarian guardian angel.

When I began an experimental treatment, my family and friends kneeled in my place at the adoration chapel. For some, this opportunity to adore our Lord changed their lives forever. Six months later, I finished the grueling treatment, but with an uncertain prognosis. *Ecce ancilla Domine,* my life and recovery were surrendered; all I needed to do was trust Him each day. When I was well enough, I resumed my weekly adoration hour, and this sacred time became an anchor point in my life, representing what was unchanging in my world.

Fast forward six years, and I am still here as proof that God's providential care can include miracles, although sometimes they are not always packaged as roses and sunshine. What I need to recall is the beautifully sacred moments of praying the Memorare in the silence of the chapel or while in the CT scan machine or when curled up in bed, racked by nausea. During those moments, I clung to Our Lady, reciting not only one Memorare but also St. Teresa of Calcutta's Flying Novena, consisting of nine Memorares and a tenth one in anticipatory thanksgiving because "it has never been known that anyone who fled to thy protection was left unaided."

I am now in remission, and God has blessed me with yet another miracle. He placed in my path a man who has also battled late-stage cancer and survived. John has given tremendous witness and led a faithful life. His strength and knowledge

————— ◇ —————

This sacred time became an anchor point in my life, representing what was unchanging in my world.

————— ◇ —————

of our Lord and the clarity he possesses after having been given a glimpse of heaven brings me comfort, as uncertainty still causes fear in my walk toward eternity.

We were married in Christ the King Catholic Church, next to the adoration chapel, and we now make this journey together realizing God is using us as visible signs of His love and mercy. The adoration chapel has become the hub from which I send to heaven the prayers of so many who have come to know about our miraculous recovery. They ask us to offer up intercession for themselves or their loved ones. As I kneel before Jesus in adoration and reflect on my healing, I am more thankful for the spiritual healing of my soul that came with thorns embedded in the miracle that God chose to bestow on me. *Ecce ancilla Domine!*

Jane Mooney, Daphne, AL

Pause and Pray before the Blessed Sacrament— A Sign of Hope

"May it be it done unto me according to your Word."

Luke 1:38

"Adoration is a little drop of eternity."

Cardinal Robert Sarah (2017, 99)

For Reflection

In our suffering, Jesus draws us closer to Himself. We are given a broader view of life and greater strength to carry life's burdens if we lean into Him. Our prayers of surrender and trust can pierce the barriers of time and space.

As you carry your emotional, physical, or spiritual cross, lean on our Eucharistic Lord and allow Him to refresh you.

༄ 18 ༄ *A Second Chance*

I sat in on the last informational meeting for adorers and guardians signing up for Eucharistic Adoration and tried to convince myself I was too busy to make a weekly commitment of that kind. As I listened to a chapel coordinator describe the miracles and blessings that come from spending time with Jesus in Eucharistic Adoration, my mind mocked the words, and I found myself asking, "What is she selling, modern indulgences?" Despite my lack of faith, I signed up to become a weekly adorer at two o'clock every morning, but kept silent about it to most of my family and all my friends. I did not share with anyone about my early morning holy hours with Jesus in case they perceived me to be a religious fanatic. I just went.

Jesus, however, had much greater things planned for me. There, in front of Him, I felt real peace flooding my soul and a softening of my heart taking place. Gradually my faith was renewed, my doubts were quelled, and I longed to spend time with Him. What a transformation! Jesus literally replaced my skepticism with a true understanding of adoration. I now loved going!

A brief time later, I became ill with the flu and COVID. My condition deteriorated rapidly, and I was placed on life support with a 2% chance of survival. Final preparations were made for me, my wedding ring was taken off my finger and given to my wife, and I was administered last rites. A good friend organized a prayer vigil at the adoration chapel during my beloved holy hour to storm the gates of heaven for my life. During this two o'clock vigil, my doctor was powerfully inspired to try an experimental treatment contrary to medical practice: a lung wash. It worked! Shortly thereafter, I was removed from life support and have since made a full recovery.

Before becoming an adorer, I was skeptical and mocked the miracles I had heard about regarding Divine Mercy being real, prayer being powerful, and miracles happening when people pray in adoration. Now I have experienced the mercy of Jesus for myself, and I am grateful Jesus called me to Him—doubts, questions, and all—for He gave me the biggest miracle ever: a second chance at life.

Tim Anderson, Mobile, AL

Pause and Pray before the Blessed Sacrament— A Second Chance

"Taste and see that the Lord is good; blessed is the man who takes refuge in Him."

Psalm 34:9

"When, in Adoration, we look at the consecrated Host, the Son of creation speaks to us. And so, we encounter the greatness of His gift, but we also encounter the Passion, the Cross of Jesus, and His Resurrection. Through this gaze of Adoration, He draws us toward Himself, within His mystery, through which he wants to transform us as He transformed the Host."

Benedict XVI (2006)

For Reflection

Ours is the True Church, an endless source of renewal and new beginnings. When we experience moments of doubt or disbelief, even the smallest step of faith opens the door to new understanding and transformation. What a great blessing and huge relief to be given a second chance, especially when all seems lost.

Pause before our Lord and pray for an increase in faith and charity. Thank Him for the teachings of Scripture and His church. Ask Him for help with disbelief, particularly in moments of doubt or despair. "Lord, I believe, help my unbelief" (*Mark 9:24*).

☙ 19 ☙ *Surrender*

Early one spring morning, I sat in the front pew of the adoration chapel, wanting to be as close to the Lord as possible. Listening to the Surrender Novena playing through my ear pods, I sat praying and quietly weeping over the plight of my youngest son, Joseph. The prayer's words "O Jesus, I surrender myself to you, take care of everything" held significant meaning as I prayed for Joseph's soul. A month earlier, he had experienced a sudden heart attack and, since then, he had been hospitalized in critical condition, suffering from brain damage.

——— ◇ ———

I knew the Holy Spirit's love and never-ending mercy for Joseph and for all souls who surrender to Him.

——— ◇ ———

Unsure of the outcome of his condition, my wife and I attended to his spiritual needs without delay and requested that anointing be administered to him by our parish priest. Surrendering to God's plan, we were blessed with a little over two more weeks with Joseph before God called him home. During this difficult time, I leaned heavily on our Lord with a trusting, steadfast spirit. Before leaving the Blessed Sacrament Chapel one morning, I knelt and bowed again in surrender.

Immediately, the Holy Spirit drew up in my thoughts the hours of fervent prayer offered for Joseph, the daily offering of the Mass by my wife and me, and the thousands of prayers prayed with faith by our parish family and my Cursillo Reunion group—all for Joseph's soul! *Surely*, I thought, *the Lord has spoken to me about Joseph through the blessing of these holy offerings.*

Now ready for Mass, I rose from prayer. Together, a friend and I left the chapel and walked toward the church. My friend was excited and wanted to share with me what he had experienced as we adored on this particular morning. He told me he had felt Jesus's Presence intensely in the chapel, whispering in his ear exactly the thoughts of my mind as I had been kneeling in prayer. At that moment, consoled and affirmed by my friend's words, I knew the Holy Spirit's love and never-ending mercy for Joseph and for all souls who surrender to Him.

Richard Givens, Daphne, AL

Pause and Pray before the Blessed Sacrament— Surrender

"So let us confidently approach the throne of grace to receive mercy and to find grace for timely help."

Hebrews 4:16

"The one who is the bread is also the mountain.... On this mountain dwells whoever has given himself to God."

St. Augustine (Becklo 2022, 170)

For Reflection

All of us are indeed pilgrims passing through this earthly life. If we strive to love the Lord with all our hearts, we will be able to allow Him to hold us and love us in times of deep sorrow.

Pray today for the grace to give yourself and all that belongs to you entirely to the Lord. When you reach that total surrender, you will then know peace and joy beyond all telling.

❦ 20 ❦ *Ladder of Miracles*

Christ the King's Blessed Sacrament Chapel is my personal weekly pilgrimage. For me, spending a weekly hour with Christ has been a gateway for opening my life to God's light and divine healing. Years ago, during my first night in the chapel, I was at peace and in prayer. The farthest thing from my mind was my father. He had initiated an extremely hurtful fight with me some months earlier and, since then, I had cut off our communication. I simply discounted him, not thinking about or talking to him since that day.

That night in the chapel, however, thoughts of my father emerged from the shadows of my mind. Thinking of him was not what I intended, nor what I wanted to pray about, yet there he was in the middle of them. All at once, disrupting this train of thought, I experienced an interior voice speaking to me: "Forgive him."

I was dumbfounded. Then I became incredibly emotional.

Unexpected grace broke through a barrier I had erected in my heart. I clearly saw the darkness festering in the relationship between us needing the cleansing light of Christ cast upon it. So, sitting there in front of Jesus, I invited Him into the situation, although forgiveness seemed so impossible. The wounds were deep, and I honestly felt it harmful to carry the relationship with my father any further, yet the words "forgive him" compelled me to move forward and alter the situation, hopefully creating a better outcome.

I struggled with forgiveness, yet over time the weekly touch of God's light in adoration chased away the shadows, causing a conversion of my behavior, actions, and thoughts. Because of this, the turmoil of other internal and external conflicts, not only the one involving my father, was resolved and restored. I am most grateful for His mercy and help in altering

— ◊ —

Unexpected grace had broken through a barrier I had erected in my heart.

— ◊ —

my bearing, for it made the impossible possible. True forgiveness was the first rung on a ladder of miracles for me. Weekly adoration has been an incredible blessing.

Joseph Buschell, Bay Minette, AL

Pause and Pray before the Blessed Sacrament— Ladder of Miracles

"If you forgive others their transgressions, your heavenly Father will forgive you."

Matthew 6:14

"He who knows how to forgive prepares for himself many graces from God. As often as I look upon the cross, so often will I forgive with all my heart."

St. Faustina Kowalska (2003, 175)

For Reflection

We cannot live at peace without seeking forgiveness. Neither can we grow in holiness. To move toward forgiveness is an act of the will and cannot happen apart from Christ. It is an act of the will and cannot happen apart from Christ. This transformative mindset, led by His grace, proclaims the glorious renewing power of God. The impossible becomes possible.

Where do you stand with Jesus's challenging command to forgive? Talk to Him directly and ask for the grace to move beyond grievances.

Chapter Six

Miracles of Love

∽ *21* ∽ *Our Truest and Best Friend*

Before I was ordained, I heard Mother Angelica, PCPA (Poor Clares of Perpetual Adoration), offer these words about Jesus in the Blessed Sacrament; this reflection forever changed how I viewed Eucharistic adoration.

Mother Angelica had to buy new shoes, so she went out and bought them. Upon returning to Our Lady of the Angels Monastery in Birmingham, she went into the chapel where the Blessed Sacrament was exposed. She stood there before Jesus and showed Him her new shoes. "See my new shoes, Jesus." She was very proud and thankful for them.

One of the other sisters said to Mother, "But Mother, don't you think Jesus knew before you ever came into the chapel that you bought new shoes?"

Mother replied, "Yes, most certainly He knew that. In fact, He knew from all eternity that on this day, in this chapel, in Birmingham, Alabama, I would come and show Him my new shoes. Yes, He knew it, but He wants me to tell Him about my life. He is my truest and best friend; friends share with each other what is going on in life, even what others consider insignificant or boring. For Jesus, there is nothing insignificant or boring when it comes to us."

Mother's insight into the dynamism of Eucharistic Adoration was simple, yet quite profound. I know it greatly impacted me and continues to impact my time before Jesus in the Blessed Sacrament. I come before a *real* person, a real living and breathing person. As Father Paddy Maher says: "A person who is madly in love with us."

God was not content to entrust the prophets of old with His message of divine love. God Himself, in Jesus of Nazareth, came in person, in the incarnation, to not only tell us of His prodigious love, but to show us, in His crucified body His divine love. Each soul He receives is a declaration of this love. Since we were not at His cross, He comes now in person, in the Blessed Sacrament, with the same message of divine love.

He is indeed our truest and best friend, and He abides with us in the greatest of all the sacraments to speak heart to heart with us. He desperately wants to hear from us, to hear anything about our day, our joys, our sorrows, our frustrations, even about our new shoes, but He especially wants to hear of our love. He wants to hear from me, Father J. Francis Sofie, Jr., because no one but me can love Him with all my heart, my heart that loves so imperfectly. Yet as imperfect as my love is, He still wants to hear of it. Before the Blessed Sacrament, perfect love meets imperfect love so that I can, through Him, with Him, and in Him, attain the perfection of charity.

— ◇ —

Yet as imperfect as my love is, He still wants to hear of it.

— ◇ —

The Blessed Sacrament is the sacrament of Divine Love. As we share with Him from our heart, He is able to reach in and expand our hearts so that we can receive more of His divine and transforming love. The more we are filled with

His love, the more we are transformed into living images of Him. In essence, we become what we love or, I should say, we become *who* we love. Through fidelity to Eucharistic Adoration, we will be able to say with St. Paul, "I live now not I, but it is Christ, my truest and best friend, who lives in Me" (Galatians 2:20).

Reverend J. Francis Sofie, Mobile, AL

Pause and Pray before the Blessed Sacrament—
Our Truest and Best Friend

"I love you, O Lord, my strength." *Psalm 18:1*

"You heard me, only Friend whom I love.
    To ravish my heart, you became man.
You shed your blood, what a supreme mystery!
    ... And you still live for me on the Altar.
If I cannot see the brilliance of your Face,
    or hear your sweet voice,
O my God, I can live by your grace,
    I can rest on your Sacred Heart!"

St. Therese of Lisieux (Kinney 2020, 120)

For Reflection

What human friend can ever mean as much to you as Jesus? He holds you in His heart day and night. He created you and watches over you. Our identity as a child of God lies through, with, and in Him so that, as Fr. Sofie says, His perfect love meets our imperfect love and is transformed into perfection.

Write a love letter to your best friend and thank Him for His constant care. Tell Him one way you will strive to be more grateful for His friendship, such as a morning offering or night prayers.

∽22∾ *Hindsight is 20/20*

Hindsight is 20/20, so they say. My weekly visits with Jesus began in my early twenties, when I was fresh out of college. I chose the midnight hour once a week—not because I was devout, but because my social life as a young adult was so spontaneous it was the only time I could guarantee that nothing else was going on. Even then, I struggled to be consistent and awake.

Now in my early thirties, I have ten years of guardianship under my belt. During those years, Jesus has gotten me through marriage trials, fertility treatments, a failed adoption, two successful adoptions and the work on a third, potty training, hurricanes, depression, elation, surgeries, health issues, tears, pain, joy... LIFE!

> My weekly holy hour has been the backbone of my spiritual life in a powerful but subtle way.

Looking back at it all, I realize that my weekly holy hour has been the backbone of my spiritual life in a powerful but subtle way. Just as I am not aware of the vital function my physical spine performs on a moment-to-moment basis, so too has adoration been for my spiritual life. During the 2020 COVID shutdown, when I was unable to see Jesus in the Blessed Sacrament, I felt severely jarred—paralyzed even. I missed the holiness surrounding

His Presence, the inexplicable peace, the absolute silence, the feeling of safety, as though I were a child again in my dad's lap.

My 20/20 hindsight helped me see that adoring Jesus in the Blessed Sacrament is an indispensable part of my life. Beginning as a sacrifice, it has become a joy and privilege. I look forward to many more moonlit nights with Jesus.

Keri Buhring, Daphne, AL

Pause and Pray before the Blessed Sacrament— Hindsight is 20/20

"For You are with me." *Psalm 23:4*

"I saw that for us He is everything that is good, comforting, and helpful. He is our clothing, who, for love, wraps us up, holds us close; He entirely encloses us for tender love, so that He may never leave us, since He is the source of all good things for us."

Blessed Julian of Norwich (De Sola Chervin 2003, 75–6)

For Reflection

Going to adoration with a heart full of praise results in interior sanctification. To become holy is to become a saint. We were created to adore. His grace changes us inwardly. When it is nurtured before Jesus in the atmosphere of adoration, His grace is carried out into the world.

Spend time before the Blessed Sacrament and reflect on ways your interior progress has been strengthened by going to adoration often. In what ways have you advanced? For example, an increased sense of awe and wonder, peace, the ability to look beyond yourself, more frequent confession, falling in love with Jesus. Then offer Him thanks and praise for the gift of frequent adoration.

❦ *23* ❦ *Never Alone*

My precious husband Wayne introduced me to the Catholic faith when we were dating. I had been raised in a devout Baptist family and had a deep love of God, but converting to the Catholic faith opened my eyes to so much more that Jesus wanted to give me and all of us.

Wayne had many spine problems requiring multiple surgeries. He lived with more pain every day than most people realized, but his deep faith and attendance at daily Mass was what got him through. In July 2020, he fell and was totally paralyzed. He died seven weeks later. During that time, due to COVID, I couldn't be next to him in his hospital room, but I visited him every day, sitting outside his hospital window. Via FaceTime, I was able to talk and pray with him and thank him for our beautiful family and for introducing me to our Catholic faith. After hours at his window, the heat would become too much, and I would drive home praying, often going directly to our adoration chapel to sit before our Lord. I missed Wayne and dancing around the kitchen in his loving arms. I missed all the cherished moments of our life together, good and bad. I wondered who I would be without him. As I was in the chapel one day, it came to me that I would always be a child of God, never having to face anything alone.

In *John 6:68–69*, Jesus asked the disciples, "Will you also go away?"

Simon Peter replied, "Lord, to whom shall we go? You have the words of eternal life and we have believed."

I, too, believe that Jesus is living and present in the Blessed Eucharist. He is the Holy One of God, and I am never alone.

Carole Jones, Daphne, AL

Pause and Pray before the Blessed Sacrament— Never Alone

"This is how we know that we remain in Him and He is in us, that He has given us of His Spirit.... Whoever acknowledges that Jesus is the Son of God, God remains in him, and he in God."

1 John 4:13, 15

"Our Lord does not come down from Heaven every day to lie in a golden ciborium. He comes to find another heaven which is infinitely dearer to Him—the heaven of our souls."

St. Therese of Lisieux (De Sola Chervin 2003, 80)

For Reflection

God's love is most clearly seen on the cross. Carole leaned on the Lord in the most difficult of times, drawing strength from His Presence in adoration. As a result, she did not become overwhelmed by sadness and suffering, but rather she was able to reflect on her life, finding comfort and even joy in the goodness and beauty of human relationships. We are never alone. In the midst of our heaviest crosses, He is near, in our soul in grace.

Pause in prayer and weigh the precariousness of the human condition. Then balance the goodness of your life and relationships against it. Do sorrow and suffering lead you closer to God or farther away?

❦24❧ *Date Nights*

My husband and I have been blessed to have adoration (usually perpetual) everywhere we have lived over the past thirty-two years. We always loved our individual hours; they provided treasured alone time during our full life raising eight kids. But when our eldest was old enough to babysit, we took the advice of a friend and joined our holy hours to face the teenage years together, asking for God's divine help!

It has been about seventeen years since our adoration "date nights" began, and we truly hate to miss one. Most weeks it is our only guaranteed time alone together, and we usually have the chapel to ourselves, as our hour is at eight o'clock on Saturday evenings. We love to whisper our rosary together, joining our prayer of petition and thanksgiving for the week. Any difficulties or frustrations troubling us dissolve quickly, as we present ourselves in solidarity before our Lord, and we leave every visit united, strengthened, and peaceful.

We give our Lord in the Blessed Sacrament credit for countless graces and gifts over the years. There has been no unanswered prayer of difficulty that we haven't been able to face with His aid. There is a true relationship of the "three of us" after so many evenings spent together. Even those weeks when we are tired or distracted, God consistently proves that He can't be outdone in generosity.

Our dream is to one day live close enough to our adoration chapel to be able to walk there so that, even in our old age, we will be able to easily go and pray for our children and grandchildren—especially as the next generation enters those same teenage years!

Marguerite Murphy, Daphne, AL

Pause and Pray before the Blessed Sacrament— Date Nights

"I love you, Lord, my strength."   *Psalm 18:1*

"Cast yourself into the arms of God and be very sure that if He wants anything of you, He will fit you for the work and give you strength."

St. Philip Neri (De Sola Chervin 2003, 62)

For Reflection

When couples learn to unite in prayer before our Eucharistic Lord, grace and blessings abound! As they place their hope and confidence in Christ alone, their everyday trials and burdens are lightened as an offering to the Lord.

Please pray for more engaged and married couples to consecrate and commit themselves to a shared holy hour.

❧25❧ *Just Be*

Sharon

I love going to adoration and being present with our Eucharistic Lord and He with me. It is a time of quiet solitude that beautifully complements my introverted personality. Sometimes I pray the Rosary, read a spiritual book, or write in my journal. Other times, I simply sit in His Presence, thanking Him for my blessings. I bring Him my needs, worries, and concerns. I listen and ask Him to speak to my mind and heart, providing me His grace and guidance. I always leave feeling peaceful and reassured. Once my little five-year-old granddaughter accompanied me to adoration and experienced her own holy moment with God. We had been to morning Mass, and she was hesitant about spending another quiet hour in church, when I told her we were going to adore Jesus. I had brought paper and crayons with me, thinking that might occupy her. After we sat down, she quickly became absorbed in her artwork. When we got up to leave, she was anxious to show me what she had drawn—a beautifully detailed picture of the altar and monstrance. What a gift to me, God, and herself! I knew He was pleased with her hour with Him, and I hope she will always remember how she felt that day in His Presence.

Charles

Sharon loves adoration, and I remember vividly the first time she invited me to go with her. I had yet to experience her peacefulness, as my extroverted personality tends toward talking and doing rather than being quiet and in stillness. Maybe, I thought, adoration is only for solemn, holy people. If I went, I might not hear any revelation from God! However, as the holy hour began, I closed my eyes, and a sense of release came over me. Never had I experienced such calmness and peace! In letting go of my expectations and letting God lead my soul, I realized the true blessing of what it is to just be with Him. Then He takes care of the rest.

Charles and Sharon Pinkert, Robertsdale, AL

Pause and Pray before the Blessed Sacrament— Just Be

"Behold, the Lamb of God who takes away the sin of the world."

John 1:29

"Every moment of prayer, especially before Our Lord in the tabernacle, is a sure, positive gain. The time we spend in daily audience with God is the most precious part of the whole day."

St. Teresa of Kolkata (Becklo 2022, 197–8)

For Reflection

In the business of life, there is a place for fleeting prayers and quick aspirations, but there is also a need for prayerful silence and contemplative slowness. To feel what it is like to linger with Jesus and just be, in His house, surrounded by His grace, is humbling and awe inspiring!

Linger with Jesus in adoration for a while and share with Him your ordinary and extraordinary concerns, circumstances, and joys. Then, be still, be quiet, and experience what it is to listen, to soak in His love, and to just be.

❧ 26 ❧ *Whispers from God*

My one word for adoration is "peace." My experience in adoration has not been one great big, huge "God moment"; rather, it has been made up of many, many small peaceful moments spent with God.

At first, when I thought about dedicating an hour each week to adoration, I was worried about whether I could keep the commitment long term, but that has not been a problem. My husband and I adore together as a couple, and it is a special blessing to spend time together in prayer with Jesus. Adoration has become a top priority in our lives.

The other concern I had when beginning adoration was how to fill the hour. Again, this has not been an issue at all. I begin by bringing to Jesus in prayer each person in my immediate family by name: my husband, children and their spouses, grandchildren, parents, brothers, sisters, extended family, friends, and so on. Then I move on to the people I know who are sick, who need prayer, or who have asked for prayer. Periodically, when I am asked to pray for someone's specific need, those requests pop into my mind and are offered to our Lord. I also like to pray the Rosary, read Scripture, or work on my Bible study material. Occasionally, I read spiritual books, but most importantly, I just sit and listen. I believe that in adoration we receive many whispers from God as to His will and direction for our lives and answers to life's questions. I sometimes ask for things, but mostly, I thank God for the many blessings in my life.

The adoration chapel at Christ the King is beautiful.

It is not ornate, but simple and humble. Years from now, I truly believe the chapel will be remembered as a peaceful and comforting place for everyone to encounter Jesus. I know it has been for me.

Lisa Boos, Daphne, AL

Pause and Pray before the Blessed Sacrament— Whispers from God

"Have no anxiety at all, but in everything, by prayer and petition, with thanksgiving, make your requests known to God. Then the peace of God that surpasses all understanding will guard your hearts and minds in Christ Jesus."

Philippians 4:6–7

"Trust filled prayer is a response of the heart open to encouraging God face to face, where all is peaceful, and the quiet voice of the Lord can be heard in the midst of silence."

Pope Francis (2018)

For Reflection

Prayer is lifting our thoughts and our will to God. The Catechism clearly defines prayer as a "vital and personal relationship with the living and true God" (United States Catholic Conference 2007, 2258). It rises from the heart turned to God in a longing to grow closer to Him and involves both speaking and listening. Each person has his or her own personal touch in drawing nearer to God in gratitude, respect, sorrow, and desire.

God is always reaching out to us; prayer is our response. Decide what part of your day is most appropriate for being still in the presence of God and then commit to regular visits with Him.

Chapter Seven

Miraculous Signs and
Wonders

❧27❧ *A Supernatural Light*

I, my wife, and three other adorers were in the chapel late one midsummer afternoon. During the hour, I was distracted by a peculiar event occurring in the tabernacle below the monstrance. There was a strange light running up and down and across the top and bottom of the tabernacle on the brass trim of the door. I was literally fixated on this strange light and wondered from where it was coming. There was a large window at the back of the altar made of muted glass. However, even if light filtered in from that window, it could not have presented itself in front of the tabernacle. I briefly suspected that an adventuresome teenager had slipped into the back of the chapel and was shining a laser light pen up and down the sides of the tabernacle, but when I turned to look, I saw that no one new had entered.

The light continued for about four or five minutes and then abruptly stopped. Almost immediately after the cessation of light traveling around the trim of the door, another light appeared from the interior of the tabernacle and began pulsating through the cross on the tabernacle door. Astounded, I turned to my wife and asked, "Do you see what is going on with the tabernacle?" She had been deeply engrossed in reading her Bible and had not noticed anything, but then the adorer behind me said, "I saw it!" For a moment I thought I had imagined the whole episode until the other adorer confirmed she had seen it too. After witnessing this phenomenon of light, I don't believe that either of us had any doubts that Jesus, the Light of the world, was indeed in the tabernacle.

Dr. Christopher Welch, Fairhope, AL

Pause and Pray before the Blessed Sacrament— A Supernatural Light

"I am the light of the world. Whoever follows me will not walk in darkness but will have the light of life."

John 8:12

"In your light you have made me know your truth: You are that light beyond all light who gives the mind's eye supernatural light in such fullness and perfection that you bring clarity even to the light of faith. In that faith I see that my soul has life, and in that light receives you who are light. Amen."

St. Catherine of Siena (1980, 364–5)

For Reflection

Jesus gives to our mind great thoughts and sheds light on our narrow earthly views. He desires us to come to Him in trust. Signs and wonders don't always accompany our interactions with the Blessed Sacrament, yet at times they can.

Resolve to visit our Eucharistic Lord more regularly— not for outward signs, but for inner grace and peace.

‿✄28✄‿ *A Heavenly Gift*

During my adoration hour, I happened to be the only guardian in the chapel. I was very troubled and was talking to Jesus about my daughter. Humble and honest, I poured out my soul in fervent prayer. Like the biblical Hannah, the more I shared with Him, the more emotional I became. I was grateful to be alone. I was sitting in the first pew in front of the statue of Our Lady. So strong in my heart was the desire to be physically closer to her Son that I moved in front of the altar and knelt before Him on the floor.

Tears streaming down my face, I left nothing unsaid in my anguish. Before long I experienced something stronger fortifying my heart: a great sense of trust that God indeed had a path for my child and I need not be afraid.

> Like Hannah, I was able to leave the chapel in peace.

In that moment of obedience, I was finally able to surrender the situation to Him. I turned back to Our Lady and asked if she would wrap her comforting arms around my daughter. Immediately, I felt the burden lift. Imagine my surprise when I rose from the floor and moved back to my pew to find a beautiful blue rosary right where I had been sitting only moments earlier. The rosary had not been there when I knelt on the floor, and I was a bit confused at first. Perhaps Mother Mary had placed it there for me to find. Or maybe my guardian angel had done it on her behalf. Nonetheless, I understood it to be confirmation that my prayers were heard and, like Hannah, I was able to leave the chapel in peace.

Since that day, I have found it much easier to release my children and grandchildren to our Lord. It gives me immeasurable hope to remember that He loves them and longs for them even more than I do. The rosary I keep on my nightstand. My prayers for my child are tucked within its beads as a reminder that I always have a loving Mother who cares deeply for me and understands a mother's hurt for her children. She prays with me and brings me to her Son.

Jan Shadis, Bay Minette, AL

Pause and Pray before the Blessed Sacrament— A Heavenly Gift

"Behold, I stand at the door and knock."
Revelation 3:20

"The interior life is like a sea of love in which the soul is plunged and is, as it were, drowned in love. Just as a mother holds her child's face in her hands to cover it with kisses, so does God hold the devout soul."
St. John Vianney (De Sola Chervin 2003, 79)

For Reflection

Releasing our loved ones is never easy. We forget that they were entrusted to us by our Creator, and He loves them more deeply than we do. His generosity and goodness never turn away from any of us.

When you make your next visit to the church or adoration chapel, physically hold out your hands and give your loved ones to our Eucharistic Lord. It will be an exhilarating experience!

∾29∾ *I Saw Him*

One summer evening I went to the adoration chapel carrying my journal with me as I had done each week for years. I always enjoyed talking with Jesus and His Mother through the process of writing down my thoughts and prayers. Little did I know how heart-changing and life-changing this holy hour would be.

As I made my way to my favorite pew, I paused to genuflect on both knees and glanced up to greet our Eucharistic Lord. In that moment I saw Him! I saw His face and all His features, His long hair and brilliant white robe. I looked down thinking, *Is this real?* I even tried to distract myself, but as I looked up again, His features were so clear I could not look away. I was overwhelmed with feeling and emotion.

At the time, there was another adorer in the chapel with me. A fleeting thought ran through my mind. *Did He reveal Himself to her as well?* As we left, we both walked to our cars rather quietly. After reaching them we paused and looked at each other. She asked me, "Did you see what I saw tonight?"

Without delay we started talking excitedly, sharing with each other what we had seen. It was exactly the same for both of us: His face, His features, His hair, and the brilliance of His white robe. Hugging each other and weeping, we knew in that moment what a gift we had received. I came home and journaled everything I had experienced.

All these years later, I have continued to see Him. I often ask Him and ponder why He chose me. Yet when I question it, in the same moment a calmness comes over me that surpasses all understanding of my own.

Now, I humbly bow my head and thank Him for the unimaginable gift of this miracle and for choosing me.

Stephanie Argiro, Daphne, AL

Pause and Pray before the Blessed Sacrament—I Saw Him

"Thomas answered and said to him, 'My Lord and my God.'"

John 20:28

"It seems to me I have found my heaven on earth, because my heaven is You, my God, and You are in my soul. You in me, and I in You—may this be my motto."

St. Elizabeth of the Trinity (Our Lady of Mercy Lay Carmelites 2023)

For Reflection

God has blessed us with the gifts of human reason and logic. He also allows experiences that reach beyond what we know and perceive. But truly the greatest miracle ever is that we can see Jesus through the eyes of faith. He manifests Himself magnificently in the Eucharist at Mass and in the Blessed Sacrament, but also in countless other ways day in and day out. If we have the eyes and ears of faith, we will see Him standing before us always. What a miracle that is!

While you are before Him in adoration, use your eyes and ears of faith. Reflect on your belief and desire to know Him, to know His truth, and to know His Real Presence.

❧ 30 ❧ *Charlie's Miracle*

When our first grandchild was born with the disease Pachygyria (also known as "smooth brain"), I had been the perpetual adoration chapel coordinator at Christ the King Catholic Church in Daphne, AL, for three years. As we were given the devastating news that little Charlie would never walk, talk, or sit up on his own, I heard my own son ask the neonatologist, "Will he know me? Will he know I'm his dad?"

Upon hearing the prognosis, I hurried from the NICU to the hospital chapel to pour out my heart to Jesus in His Eucharistic Presence. As I prayed, my son Chase soon joined me in the chapel.

Later that evening, in the black stillness of the hotel room, I heard within my heart, "Just ask!" So I did. In the darkness, I composed a novena prayer in praise of God's mercy. I prayed for strength for Charlie's parents, Chase and Janna, and for healing of Charlie, if it be God's holy will. The next day we shared this prayer with family, friends, neighbors, and Catholic school children as well as our 400+ chapel guardians to pray with us for the next nine days.

Many of the guardians responded immediately. One man shared that this novena was the start of his whole family praying together. Another woman, Jeanne, who had recently moved to Alabama from France, shared Charlie's novena with her mother, which prompted her mother to travel from her little French village to Lourdes at the novena's end on February 11. Jeanne's mother even sent pictures of her and her husband lighting a candle for Charlie in the Lourdes' Grotto. These were Charlie's prayer warriors, and our Eucharistic Lord in churches and chapels around the world was our link to one another as the Body of Christ.

After observing six months of steady improvement, Charlie's second MRI showed complete healing. There was no more fluid around the brain, his front atrophied lobe had grown to a normal size, and his smooth brain had developed ridges. Charlie's pediatric neurologist, a devout Catholic herself, said there was no medical explanation for Charlie's healing, but with God, all things were possible.

Jesus is who He says He is, and He can do all things. We have experienced this truth firsthand. He is still walking beside us. As a chapel coordinator for more than twelve years now, I can attest to the truth that adoration chapels are a powerhouse of prayer. Stepping from the world and into an adoration chapel feels like a transcendence of time and space. I am and will be forever grateful for His loving Presence with us. God's mercies are new every day, and He is with us until the end of the age.

I heard within my heart, "Just ask!"

Missy Treutel Schmidt, Daphne, AL

See Appendix 4 for Charlie's pictures

Pause and Pray before the Blessed Sacrament—Charlie's Miracle

"I have the strength for everything through Him who empowers me."

Philippians 4:13

"It [the Blessed Sacrament] is the center of existence for me; all the rest of life is expendable."

Flannery O'Connor (Becklo 2022, 9)

For Reflection

Jesus sees, plans, and permits all things for our truest and most lasting welfare. Intercessory prayer brought Charlie into God's healing Presence. We must always pray for the perfect ending and desire to accept His final decisions in all matters.

Place your greatest needs and desires at Jesus's feet knowing He loves you. Always end with "Thy kingdom come, Thy will be done."

Chapter Eight

Reflections from a Chapel

Coordinator

Reflections from a Chapel Coordinator

I hope you have enjoyed reading these personal encounters. My position as a chapel coordinator has given me access to many more, a few of which I want to share, as a final word, so you can understand the overwhelming richness and blessings of our parish's experience of Perpetual Eucharistic Adoration.

When the Blessed Sacrament Chapel on Main Street in Daphne was forming in 2010, we received beautiful spiritual support from a sister perpetual adoration chapel two states away at Holy Name of Jesus parish in New Orleans, LA. Mary Alice McKay, a thirty-year chapel coordinator, became a dear friend who called me each week to check on our progress, offer encouragement, and assure us of her guardian's prayers. Mary Alice even shared how their chapel had weathered Hurricane Katrina in 2005, remaining open throughout the storm and the aftermath, with men in the parish taking entire night shifts alone to stay with our Lord.

In 2019, we "prayed it forward" by doing the same for a newly forming Perpetual Eucharistic Adoration chapel in Mobile, AL. Just as Mary Alice had done, I called and encouraged the coordinators, Ines and Cathi. In addition, I asked our 500+ guardians to pray one Hail Mary at the start of their weekly visits for the St. Ignatius chapel's successful formation. Their Blessed Sacrament Chapel opened on the Feast of the Immaculate Conception on December 8, 2019. Truly, our Lord brought us all together to be part of His greater plan.

Renee Leonard shared that, when the adoration chapel was in its formation year, her husband signed up for one of the 168 hours being filled by committed adorers. However, before the chapel opened, he passed away. I called Renee a few weeks later and asked if she would prayerfully consider committing to a weekly holy hour. She explained that signing up for a holy hour was her husband's idea, not hers. At that point I asked if she would consider guardianship of an hour on a trial basis for three weeks, at which point I would check back with her to see if she wanted to continue. She reluctantly agreed. However, after just two weeks, she called me in tears and said she wanted to continue because, while in front of Jesus, she experienced feelings of great mercy and consolation in her grief. She said it felt as if there were two others present with her: Jesus Himself and her husband sitting at her side.

During our formation year, we answered requests from twelve neighboring parishes inquiring about weekly commitments for holy hours. Dawn Peterson, an elementary school teacher, signed up from her parish in Gulf Shores and drove nearly an hour one way each week for her midnight holy hour. Her non-Catholic friend, Linda, soon joined her to keep her company. Over the years, Linda sat with our Lord and read material from the chapel library; she eventually became convinced by the truth of the Catholic faith. Many of us were overjoyed to learn that Linda was received into the Catholic Church two years after she began weekly Eucharistic Adoration visits.

Each year we are grateful to introduce the blessing of adoration to RCIA classes. One year during the RCIA class at Christ the King, two candidates were so moved to learn of the power of our Eucharistic Lord that they both immediately signed up for the two o'clock night hour each week. Years later, both men expressed their joy in finding such a gift. One of the men even donated an air purification system to the chapel so we could open quickly following the COVID shutdown.

Sandra Warren and Dinnean Mattingly were unacquainted with each other and a whole generation apart in age, yet they had unknowingly selected the same ten o'clock morning holy hour. Becoming prayer partners and friends, they realized after just a few weeks that God had brought them together for a divine purpose: to intercede with zeal on behalf of their special needs children. Through the eyes of faith, these two mothers recognized their hour together in the chapel as an opportunity to gain grace and strength from Jesus and each other as they united in sincere prayer for their children.

As she was sitting in her early morning holy hour, Julie Christman had on her heart to pray for a family who had just lost their young son in a tragic ATV accident. She didn't know the family except their name and was praying for them. Just then, a man walked into the chapel. As she watched him kneel quietly at the altar in prayer, her heart—prompted by the Holy Spirit—was filled with compassion and sympathy. When the man turned to leave, she said to him in a low voice, "I am keeping you and your family in prayer," to which he replied, "Thank you. We feel them." Only later was it confirmed to her that he was indeed the father of the son who had died.

Karin Caswell shared how her time during adoration provided her with the opportunity to grow in a personal relationship with Jesus through His Word. Over the years, He has been an incredible source of comfort and strength during times of tremendous joy, suffering, and uncertainty for her. Confident that Jesus will speak to her with clarity through Sacred Scripture, Karin likes to select and meditate on a passage particular to whatever need or circumstance she may be experiencing at the moment. Her favorite verse is *John 16:33*: "I have told you this so that you might have peace in Me. In the world you will have trouble, but take courage, I have conquered the world." Karin says the greatest gift of adoration is spending time in silence and really listening for Jesus communicating through His Word because it has had an ever-deepening effect on her relationship with Him.

Cindy Teague had been the sole guardian at the adoration chapel Saturday evenings at seven o'clock for more than ten years. She was a steadfast prayer warrior and faithful to her adoration hour. One Thursday in June, she called to say that she was in the hospital with stage four cancer and had been given only a short while to live. She wanted to make sure that her adoration hour would be covered since she was alone as sole guardian. I quickly prayed to the Holy Spirit to give her words of peace and comfort, and I thanked her for her loyal love of the Lord. She passed away two days later. The following Saturday, I received a call from a couple, Jim and Kelly Bolden, who said they were ready to take an hour together and said they would take any hour that was available. They signed up for Cindy's hour. As she had requested, Cindy's seven o'clock Saturday evening holy hour was never left alone.

Irene Minto called to say she was thrilled to see that not one, but two new guardians had signed up for her ten o'clock holy hour. She had faithfully been the guardian of this evening hour on her own for nine years and had been directly praying to the Lord, asking Him for reinforcements to cover her weekly commitment before leaving due to her own illness. Irene shared that her years of weekly prayer sustained her as her daughter battled cancer at MD Anderson. For years she accompanied Karen to her treatments, and eventually her daughter was able to "ring the bell" when her treatments were complete. Irene also shared that her daughter's remission lasted a few years, but eventually her cancer returned, and her daughter died. One evening at her holy hour, as this devoted lady was pouring her heart out to Jesus and mourning her daughter's death, she heard the ringing of a bell in the chapel, clear as day. She turned to see if someone with a ringing watch or cell phone had stepped into the chapel, but no one was there. The next week during her hour with Jesus, as she was praying for her daughter, she heard a bell ring once more. This time she understood, and it gave her great peace and comfort to know her daughter was letting her know she was okay; her battle was over. Adoration gave her the peace to accept and overcome this great loss.

Monica Smith was in the chapel late one evening and experienced a remarkable vision while in prayer. She saw an exquisitely detailed image of the face of Jesus surrounded by the wings of angels running along the lower edge of the altar cloth. Adding to this extraordinary moment, Monica saw imagery of the Archangel Gabriel and the Blessed Mother. These images also exhibited minute details of the Archangel and his trumpet as well as the soft folds and ripples in the Blessed Mother's veil. Later, Monica commented, "After attending a retreat, I understood the movement of the Holy Spirit in a new way. These gifts brought me great consolation and comfort when, after seven years of weekly adoration, I had to step away from adoration to care for my sick mother."

Sandra's Aunt Frances was diagnosed and declared terminally ill, but the family was uncertain how long she had to live. One day in the chapel during her usual holy hour, Sandra experienced a vision of her aunt near the Blessed Sacrament exposed in the monstrance. Later, when she arrived home, she called her sister and asked if she had any news about Aunt Frances. Her sister replied that she did not. Shortly after their conversation, at one o'clock, her sister called again bearing the news that their aunt had just passed away. Prior to her passing, however, Aunt Frances told her son, who was with her at the time, that she was going to visit her nieces. Sandra realized that would have been exactly when she was at the adoration chapel in prayer for her. With a heart full of gratitude, Sandra gave thanks to God for a beautiful and comforting gift given to her in those sacred moments.

Deacon Ted Schmidt shared the following story: "Serving as a deacon is a precious gift I treasure. Even though I still work full time, the opportunities to serve daily Masses and assist our priests on the weekends fill me with great joy. The challenge remains, however, in finding quality time for daily prayer. And here is precisely where the beauty of an adoration chapel shines. Every hour is available for focused time with the Lord. I have found that early Sunday morning works best for me. The tranquil stillness in the presence of the Blessed Sacrament gives me clarity of mind and heart. Often, I get so caught up in prayer that I hardly notice the time has flown by. Whether I am polishing a homily or praying morning prayers from the Breviary, my holy hour allows me time to 'lean in' on Jesus and still make it in time to assist at the seven o'clock Sunday morning Mass. Indeed, my weekly holy hour with the Eucharistic Lord fuels me to serve with greater faith, hope, and love."

Paul Dowsey described his experience with a favorite physician whom he admires very much. He said that, during his appointments, he can immediately feel her calming presence; as soon as she walks through the door to the exam room, his "what if" fears vanish when she greets him with a warm, assuring smile. "She exudes a demeanor of peace and comfort," Paul added, "that enables me to intuitively sense all will be well." Paul associates the same feelings of peace and comfort—only greatly magnified—with what he experiences as an adorer entering the chapel. He knows that, when he steps in, he is in the presence of Someone who is always there to greet him with a supernatural smile that radiates love and assurance. "Jesus calms my fears and removes the negative thoughts that unsettle me," Paul commented. "Again, intuitively, I know all is well if I remain with Him. He is the Greatest Physician!" (Note: This beautiful man submitted the first entry for this book. He was gentle, kind, and never missed his one o'clock Saturday morning holy hour until the day the Lord called him home. Paul lived in Westminster Village Senior Living.)

Part III
Your Miracles Await!

Chapter Nine

A Powerhouse of Grace

Hundreds of people are drawn to our chapel for personal reasons every day. Some drop in for only a few minutes; others stay for hours. They come with anxieties and distractions, sorrows and joys, each reacting to Jesus in their own unique way. After interacting with Him, they leave, taking Him out into the world, affecting change.

With the forming of Blessed Sacrament Chapel, we have seen:

- an increase in priestly and religious vocations from our parish and archdiocese,
- an increase in attendance for the Sacrament of Reconciliation, which has caused Confession hours to be extended,
- an increase in works of charity,
- an increase in babies being born to infertile mothers, and
- an increase in families being restored to a peaceful state when one or more members have turned to the Eucharistic Lord in weekly adoration.

The beauty of these chapels, which are truly spiritual powerhouses of grace, is that they can transform lives and communities to be a beacon of hope anywhere. Our chapel on Main Street in Daphne is such a helpful example because it is quite simply a "meat and potatoes" parish. It is not associated with any famous shrine and doesn't require those who pray there to make arduous pilgrimages. It is literally right around the corner and available for special, intimate encounters at any time, twenty-four hours a day, seven days a week.

It is our hope that, having read these testimonies, you will have heard Jesus calling you to sit a while each week at His side. He has so much to share with you.

Please see Appendix 1 for Establishing Your Own Perpetual Adoration Chapel.

Appendix 1

Steps to Establishing Your Perpetual Adoration Chapel

1.) Pray continually to the Holy Spirit to direct and guide you.

2.) Approach your pastor for his blessing.

3.) Place in church bulletins, Flocknotes, and Eblasts a request for volunteers from your parish (and surrounding parishes) to form a Perpetual Eucharistic Adoration (PEA) committee.

4.) Invite a visiting Eucharistic priest to promote PEA at all masses and to share about its beautiful fruits, and allow parishioners to fill out a form of interest. The goal is to collect at least 400 forms of interest.

5.) Guide your PEA committee in making phone calls to all interested parishioners, filling the 168 hours of a week.

6.) Use as your guide *Real Presence Eucharistic Education and Adoration Association PEA Manual* (**www.therealpresence. org**).

Appendix 2

How to Pray a Holy Hour, a Minute-by-Minute Guide

To pray a holy hour, all you need is a tabernacle with a lit sanctuary lamp, a Bible, and perhaps a Compendium of the Catechism of the Catholic Church (available online).

Three Rules

1. Be Silent. Don't rattle prayers or silently review stresses. Be still exteriorly and interiorly.

2. Be Attentive. It's not simply a reading hour — reading should be an entry-point to prayer.

3. Be Alert. Sit, stand, or kneel respectfully. Quick tip: If you get sleepy, stand up!

Minute-by-Minute

There is no one way to pray a holy hour. The following might help if you get lost in the hour, but feel free to reconfigure it to suit your needs.

:00-:05 – Begin

First 5 Minutes: Ask the Holy Spirit to help you, then make acts of faith, hope and charity. Tell God how you believe, trust and love him. Ask for more faith, hope and love.

Quick tip: There are great prayers to the Holy Spirit and Acts of Faith, Hope and Love in the Compendium.

:05-:15 – Adoration

Next 10 Minutes: Adore God. He holds the universe like a seed in the palm of his hand. He is all powerful, all good, more beautiful than we can imagine, and more real than the small things that we grasp so easily. Imagine Christ sitting with you.

Tell him: "Oh my God, I adore your divine greatness from the depths of my littleness; you are so great, and I am so small." or "Glory be ..." Repeat as long as necessary.

Quick Tip: Try the Te Deum in the Compendium. Scriptural helps for adoration—Exodus 33:18-23; Song of Songs 2:8-17; Matthew 2:1-11; John 1:1-18; Colossians 1:15-20; Philippians, 2:6-11.

:15-:25 – Contrition

Next 10 Minutes: Offer reparation. It's not your love for God, but his for you that saves. Examine your conscience. Offer reparation for the sins of the world. Pray: "Oh my Jesus, I am so sorry. Forgive me." (Imagine Jesus on the cross; kiss each wound.)
Quick tip: Scriptures for contrition—1Corinthians 13:4-7; Colossians 3:5-10; 1 Timothy 1:12-17; James 3:2-12; 1 John 1:5-2:6; Penitential Psalms: 6, 32, 38, 51, 102, 130, 142.

:25-:40 – Meditation

Next 15 Minutes: Contemplate God's action. You may wish to meditatively pray the Stations of the Cross or a Rosary. Or:
Scriptural meditation. Read a brief Gospel passage. Imagine the scene. Notice Christ's reactions. Think of three ways the passage applies to your own life. Meditate on each line.
Doctrinal meditation. Read Scripture or Catechism passages that apply to a doctrine of the Church. Appreciate God's plan and find ways it applies to you. (Perhaps: Sun, Resurrection; Mon, Incarnation; Tues, Mercy/confession; Wed, Holy Spirit; Thurs, Eucharist; Fri, Passion; Sat., Mary).
Life meditation. Or, deepening your examination of conscience, look at your own life. Which kind of pride do you most fall into? Selfishness (valuing yourself most), Vanity (valuing others opinions most), Sensuality (valuing comforts most). Pray for the opposite virtues: Charity (serving others first), Fidelity (putting Christ's opinion first), Discipline (accepting your crosses).

:40-:50 – Thanksgiving

Next 10 Minutes: Express gratitude for all God's gifts. He didn't just create you, he sustains your existence out of love in every moment. Thank him for literally everything, and be specific: food, shelter, clothing, health, family, friends, teachers, coworkers, home, and most of all spiritual gifts — faith, hope, love, this time of prayer, the Catholic faith, the disciples who reached you.
Thank God for answers to prayer. Thank him for crosses. Thank him for creating you and caring so much for you that he died for you.
Quick tip: Scriptures for thanksgiving – Genesis 1; Genesis 8:15-22; Job 1:13-22; Daniel 3:46 ff.; Matthew 6:25-34; Luke 17:11-19; Psalms: 8, 65, 66, 100, 111.

:50-:55 – Petition God

Next 5 Minutes: Ask God for what you and others need. He is the king of the universe. He's in control, even when it isn't obvious.

Pray for: The Church, the pope's intentions, for those who are suffering, for priests and bishops, for religious, for vocations, for your country, your family, for what you need most in the spiritual life. Pray for peace and the protection of the institution of the family. Pray for those who have asked for prayers.

:55-1:00

Final 5 Minutes: Make a resolution to act on a light of the Holy Spirit you received: something doable and checkable.

Ask the Blessed Mother to help you, perhaps with Marian prayers from the Compendium.

Appendix 3

15 Prayers of St. Bridget

St. Bridget of Sweden (1303–1373) was one of the patron saints of Europe, a mystic, and a founder of a religious order. For a long time, St. Bridget wanted to know the number of blows our Lord received during His passion. One day, He appeared to her and said: "I received 5480 blows on My Body. **If you wish to honor them in some way, say 15 Our Fathers and 15 Hail Marys with the following prayers (which He taught her) for a whole year. When the year is up, you will have honored each one of My Wounds.**"

15 Prayers of St Bridget

First Prayer: Our Father—Hail Mary

O Jesus Christ! Eternal Sweetness to those who love Thee, joy surpassing all joy and all desire, Salvation and Hope of all sinners, Who hast proved that Thou hast no greater desire than to be among men, even assuming human nature at the fullness of time for the love of men, recall all the sufferings Thou hast endured from the instant of Thy conception, and especially during Thy Passion, as it was decreed and ordained from all eternity in the Divine plan.

Remember, O Lord, that during the Last Supper with Thy disciples, having washed their feet, Thou gavest them Thy Most Precious Body and Blood, and while at the same time Thou didst sweetly console them, Thou didst foretell them Thy coming Passion.

Remember the sadness and bitterness which Thou didst experience in Thy Soul as Thou Thyself bore witness saying: "My Soul is sorrowful even unto death."

Remember all the fear, anguish and pain that Thou didst suffer in Thy delicate Body before the torment of the crucifixion, when, after having prayed three times, bathed in a sweat of blood, Thou wast betrayed by Judas, Thy disciple, arrested by the people of a nation Thou hadst chosen and elevated, accused by false witnesses, unjustly judged by three judges during the flower of Thy youth and during the solemn Paschal season.

Remember that Thou wast despoiled of Thy garments and clothed in those of derision; that Thy Face and Eyes were veiled; that Thou wast buffeted, crowned with thorns, a reed placed in Thy Hands; that Thou was crushed with blows and overwhelmed with affronts and outrages.

In memory of all these pains and sufferings which Thou didst endure before Thy Passion on the Cross, grant me before my death true contrition, a sincere and entire confession, worthy satisfaction, and the remission of all my sins. Amen.

Second Prayer: Our Father—Hail Mary

O Jesus! True liberty of angels, Paradise of delights! Remember the horror and sadness which Thou didst endure when Thy enemies, like furious lions, surrounded Thee, and by thousands of insults, spits, blows, lacerations and other unheard-of-cruelties, tormented Thee at will.

In consideration of these torments and insulting words, I beseech Thee, O my Savior, to deliver me from all my enemies, visible and invisible, and to bring me, under Thy protection, to the perfection of eternal salvation. Amen.

Third Prayer: Our Father—Hail Mary

O Jesus! Creator of heaven and earth Whom nothing can encompass or limit, Thou Who dost enfold and hold all under Thy loving power! Remember the very bitter pain Thou didst suffer when the Jews nailed Thy Sacred Hands and Feet to the Cross by blow after blow with big blunt nails, and not finding Thee in a pitiable enough state to satisfy their rage, they enlarged Thy Wounds, and added pain to pain, and with indescribable cruelty stretched Thy Body on the Cross, pulled Thee from all sides, thus dislocating Thy Limbs.

I beg of Thee, O Jesus, by the memory of this most loving suffering of the Cross, to grant me the grace to fear Thee and to love Thee. Amen.

Fourth Prayer: Our Father—Hail Mary

O Jesus! Heavenly Physician raised aloft on the Cross to heal our wounds with Thine! Remember the bruises which Thou didst suffer and the weakness of all Thy Members which were distended to such a degree that never was there pain like unto Thine. From the crown of Thy Head to the souls of Thy Feet there was not one spot on Thy Body that was not in torment; any yet, forgetting all Thy sufferings,

Thou didst not cease to pray to Thy heavenly Father for Thy enemies, saying: "Father forgive them, for they know not what they do."

Through this great mercy, and in memory of this suffering, grant that the remembrance of Thy most bitter Passion may affect in me a perfect contrition and the remission of all my sins. Amen.

Fifth Prayer: Our Father—Hail Mary

O Jesus! Mirror of eternal splendor! Remember the sadness which Thou experienced when, contemplating in the light of Thy Divinity the predestination of those who would be saved by the merits of Thy Sacred Passion, Thou didst see at the same time, the great multitude of reprobates who would be damned for their sins, and Thou didst complain bitterly of those hopeless, lost and unfortunate sinners.

Through this abyss of compassion and pity, and especially through the goodness which Thou displayed to the good thief when Thou saidst to him: "This day, thou shalt be with Me in paradise." I beg of Thee, O sweet Jesus, that at the hour of my death, Thou wilt show me mercy. Amen.

Sixth Prayer: Our Father—Hail Mary

O Jesus! Beloved and most desirable King! Remember the grief Thou didst suffer when, naked and like a common criminal, Thou was fastened and raised on the Cross, when all Thy relatives and friends abandoned Thee, except Thy beloved Mother, who remained close to Thee during Thy agony and whom Thou didst entrust to Thy faithful disciple when Thou saidst to Mary: "Woman, behold thy son!" and to St. John: "Son, behold thy Mother!"

I beg of Thee, O my Saviour, by the sword of sorrow which pierced the soul of Thy holy Mother, to have compassion on me in all my afflictions and tribulations, both corporal and spiritual, and to assist me in all my trials, and especially at the hour of my death. Amen.

Seventh Prayer: Our Father—Hail Mary

O Jesus! Inexhaustible Fountain of compassion, Who by a profound gesture of love said from the Cross: "I thirst!", suffered from the thirst for the salvation of the human race.

I beg of Thee, O my Savior, to inflame in my heart the desire to tend toward perfection in all my acts, and to extinguish in me the concupiscence of the flesh and the ardor of worldly desires. Amen.

Eighth Prayer: Our Father—Hail Mary

O Jesus! Sweetness of hearts, delight of the spirit! By the bitterness of the vinegar and gall which Thou didst taste on the Cross for love of us, grant me the grace to receive worthily Thy Precious Body and Blood during my life and at the hour of my death that they may serve as a remedy and consolation for my soul. Amen

Ninth Prayer: Our Father—Hail Mary

O Jesus! Royal virtue, joy of the mind! Recall the pain Thou didst endure when plunged in an ocean of bitterness at the approach of death, insulted, outraged by the Jews, Thou didst cry out in a loud voice that Thou was abandoned by Thy Father, saying: "My God, My God, why hast Thou forsaken me?"

Through this anguish, I beg of Thee O my Saviour, not to abandon me in the terrors and pains of my death. Amen.

Tenth Prayer: Our Father—Hail Mary

O Jesus! Who are the beginning and end of all things, life and virtue! Remember that for my sake Thou were plunged in an abyss of suffering from the soles of Thy Feet to the crown of Thy Head. In consideration of the enormity of Thy Wounds, teach me to keep, through pure love, Thy Commandments, whose way is wide and easy for those who love Thee. Amen.

Eleventh Prayer: Our Father—Hail Mary

O Jesus! Deep abyss of mercy! I beg of Thee, in memory of Thy Wounds which penetrated to the very marrow of Thy Bones and to the depth of Thy Being, to draw me, a miserable sinner overwhelmed by my offenses, away from sin and to hide me from thy Face justly irritated against me. Hide me in Thy Wounds until Thy anger and just indignation shall have passed away. Amen.

Twelfth Prayer: Our Father—Hail Mary

O Jesus! Mirror of truth, symbol of unity, link of charity! Remember the multitude of wounds with which Thou was covered from Head to Foot, torn and reddened by the spilling of Thy adorable Blood. O great and Universal Pain which Thou didst suffer in Thy virginal Flesh for love of us! Sweetest Jesus! What is there that Thou couldst have done for us which Thou has not done?

May the fruit of Thy sufferings be renewed in my soul by the faithful remembrance of Thy Passion and may Thy Love increase in my heart each day, until I see Thee in eternity, Thou who are the treasury of every real good and every joy, which I beg Thee to grant me, O Sweetest Jesus, in heaven. Amen.

Thirteenth Prayer: Our Father—Hail Mary

O Jesus! Strong Lion, Immortal and Invincible King! Remember the pain which Thou didst endure! When all Thy strength, both moral and physical, was entirely exhausted, Thou didst bow Thy Head, saying: "It is consummated!" Through this anguish and grief, I beg of Thee, Lord Jesus, to have mercy on me at the hour of my death when my mind will be greatly troubled and my soul will be in anguish. Amen.

Fourteenth Prayer: Our Father—Hail Mary

O Jesus! Only Son of the Father, Splendor and Figure of His Substance! Remember the simple and humble recommendation Thou didst make of Thy Soul to Thy Eternal Father, saying: "Father, into Thy Hands commend My Spirit!" And with Thy Body all torn and Thy Heart broken, and the bowels of Thy Mercy open to redeem us, Thou didst expire.

By this Precious Death, I beg of Thee, O King of Saints, to comfort me and help me to resist the devil, the fleshy and the world, so that being dead to the world I may love for Thee alone. I beg of Thee at the hour of my death to receive me, a pilgrim and an exile returning to Thee. Amen.

Fifteenth Prayer: Our Father—Hail Mary

O Jesus! True and fruitful Vine! Remember the abundant outpouring of Blood which Thou didst so generously shed from Thy Sacred Body, as juice from grapes in a wine press.

From Thy Side, pierced with a lance by a soldier, blood and water issued forth until there was not left in Thy Body a single drop; and finally, like a bundle of myrrh lifted to the top of the Cross, Thy delicate Flesh was destroyed, the very Substance of Thy Body withered, and the Marrow of Thy Bones dried up.

Through this bitter Passion and through the outpouring of Thy Precious Blood, I beg of Thee, O Sweet Jesus, to receive my soul when I am in my death agony. Amen.

Conclusion

O Sweet Jesus! Pierce my heart so that my tears of penitence and love will be my bread day and night. May I be converted entirely to Thee; may my heart be pleasing to Thee; and may the end of my life be so praiseworthy that I may merit heaven and there with Thy saints praise Thee forever. Amen.

Appendix 4

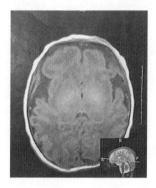

Brain scan at birth

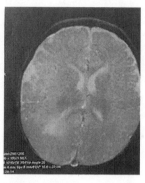

Brain scan about 6 months later

Charlie at age 3

Prayers and candles for Charlie at Lourdes, France

Blessed Sacrament Catholic Chapel
Main Street, Daphne, AL

Exterior   Interior

Blessed Sacrament Catholic Church
Omaha, NE

Kathy's Castle

Exterior   Interior

Appendix 5
What is Perpetual Eucharistic Adoration?

As Catholics we believe that "the Eucharistic Presence of Christ begins at the moment of the consecration and endures as long as the Eucharistic species subsist" (United States Catholic Conference 2007, 1377). This means that, as long as the sacred host is intact and possesses the physical properties of bread, the Real Presence of Jesus Christ—Body, Blood, Soul, and Divinity—remains.

On account of this reality, Philip Kosloski (2017), spiritual writer for Aleteia.org, said the Church started using a tabernacle (typically a gold box) as a way to protect any consecrated hosts not consumed at Mass. The Eucharistic hosts are typically stored in the tabernacle, which is marked by a red lamp that stays lit as long as there are hosts within.

Kosloski also explained the origin of Perpetual Eucharistic Adoration. He shares that, in the fifteenth century, there arose in popularity a practice that placed a host not in the tabernacle, but in a gold receptacle called a "monstrance." This device put the host on display in a clear piece of glass, surrounded by gold. Instead of being hidden away in the tabernacle, a host in the monstrance could be clearly seen and venerated by all. The purpose of this practice, according to Kosloski, centered on the desire of Christians to adore the king of kings in the sacred host and provided Christians the opportunity to have a face-to-face conversation with God, truly present in the Eucharist.

Soon, various religious orders and societies took as their

mission the perpetual adoration of Jesus in the Eucharist. They placed the monstrance on an altar and took turns adoring our Lord around the clock, ensuring that a person was accompanying the Blessed Sacrament every hour of the day. This practice has been taken up by the laity in what are now called perpetual adoration chapels. John Paul II (2003), in his encyclical *Ecclesia de Eucharistia*, exhorted pastors to "encourage, also by their personal witness, the practice of Eucharistic Adoration, and exposition of the Blessed Sacrament in particular, as well as prayer of adoration before Christ present under the Eucharistic species" (2003). At an International Eucharistic Congress in Seville, he further stated that "I hope this form of perpetual adoration, with permanent exposition of the Blessed Sacrament…results in the establishment of Perpetual Eucharistic Adoration in all parishes and Christian communities throughout the world" (1993).

Kosloski shared the practice of Eucharistic Adoration only makes sense in light of the Catholic understanding of the Eucharistic as the Real Presence of Jesus. (*John: 6*). Catholics believe that Jesus is truly there, in a special way, not found anywhere else in the world. Kosloski concluded with a short story from the life of St. Teresa of Avila that perfectly summarizes the reasoning behind Eucharistic Adoration.

One day, St. Teresa heard someone say, "If only I had lived at the time of Jesus…. If only I had seen Jesus…. If only I had talked with Jesus."

She responded, "But do we not have in the Eucharist the living, true and real Jesus present before us? Why look for more?"

With the availability of perpetual adoration, we can spend time—any time, any day—with Jesus.

Sources

August, Matthew. 2022. "From Heiress to God's Servant: St. Katharine Drexel." 5/5/2023. https://marian.org/articles/heiress-gods-servant-st-katharine-drexel

Becklo, Matthew. 2022. *The Holy Hour: Meditations for Eucharistic Adoration*. Park Ridge, IL: Word on Fire.

Benedict XVI. 2006. "Holy Mass and Eucharistic Procession on the Solemnity of the Sacred Band Blood of Christ." 7/20/2023. https://www.vatican.va/content/benedict-xvi/en/homilies/2006/documents/hf_ben-xvi_hom_20060615_corpus-christi.html

Bridget of Sweden. 2023. "15 Prayers of St. Bridget." 5/5/2023. www.ewtn.com/catholicism/library/prayers-of-saint-bridget-9117

Burkepile, Jacqueline. 2019. "Who Will Save Our Future Church?" 10/3/2023. https://www.churchpop.com/who-will-save-our-future-church-abp-fulton-sheen-nails-it-with-this-one-powerful-quote/

Carpenter, Humphrey, ed. 2012. *The Letters of J.R.R. Tolkien*. New York: Harper Collins.

Catherine of Siena. 1980. *Catherine of Siena: The Dialogue*. New York: Paulist Press.

De Sales, Francis. 2012. *Introduction to the Devout Life*. Philadelphia, PA: Tan Publishing.

De Sola Chervin, Ronda. 2003. *Quotable Saints*. Ann Arbor, MI: Servant.

Francis. 2018. "Apostolic Exhortation Gaudete et Exsultate of the Holy Father Francis on the Call to Holiness in Today's World." 5/5/2023 https://www.vatican.va/content/francesco/en/apost_exhortations/documents/papa-francesco_esortazione-ap_20180319_gaudete-et-exsultate.html

Faustina Kowalska, Maria. 2003. *Diary: Divine Mercy in My Soul*. Stockbridge, MA: Marian Press.

Hoopes, Tom. 2012. "How to Pray a Holy Hour." 8/22/2023. https://www.thegregorian.com/wp-content/uploads/2012/12/How_to_Pray_a_Holy_Hour.pdf

Guardini, Romano. 1937. *The Lord*. Southlake, TX: Gateway Editions.

John Paul II. 1999. "Apostolic Journey to America Eucharistic Celebration." 7/25/2023. https://www.vatican.va/content/john-paul-ii/en/homilies/1999/documents/hf_jp-ii_hom_19990127_stlouis.html

John Paul II. 2003. *Ecclesia de Eucharistia*. Downers Grove, IL: Intravarsity Press

John Paul II. 1993. "To the National Delegates taking part in the International Eucharistic Congress." International Eucharistic Congress, Seville, Spain.

Kinney, Donald, trans. 2020. *The Poetry of St. Therese of Lisieux*. Washington, DC: ICS.

Kosloski, Philip. 2017 What is Eucharistic Adoration? 7/2/2023. https://aleteia.org/2017/05/18/perpetual-adoration-the-closest-thing-to-walking-with-jesus/

Our Lady of Mercy Lay Carmelites. 2023. "St. Elizabeth of the Trinity." 9/15/2023. https://www.olmlaycarmelites.org/saints/st-elizabeth-trinity

Pitre, Brant. 2015. *Eucharist: Discovering the Mass in the Bible, Study Guide*. Greenwood Village, CO: Augustine Institute.

Ryan, John K. 1972. *Introduction to the Devout Life*. New York. Doubleday.

Sarah, Robert. 2017. *The Power of Silence, Against the Dictatorship of Noise*. San Francisco, CA: Ignatius Press. First Edition (March 23, 2017), p. 99

Scheenstra, Vicki. n.d. "Prayers, Quips and Quotes: St. Bridget of Sweden, Feast Day July 23." 5/5/2023. https://catholicfaithpatronsaints.com/prayers-quips-and-quotes-st-bridget-of-sweden-feast-day-july-23/

Sheen, Fulton J. 2018. *Life of Christ*. San Francisco, CA: Ignatius Press.

Senior, Donald, ed. 1990. *The Catholic Study Bible: The New American Bible* (Rev. ed.). New York: Oxford University Press.

Stephen, Ofomah. 2021. "Catholic Saints Quotes about Prayer." 8/22/2023. https://amcatholic4life.com/catholic-saints-quotes-about-prayer/

The Catholic Storeroom. n.d. "Complete Spiritual Dryness…." 8/22/2023.
https://www.catholicstoreroom.com/2017/03/30/complete-spiritual-
dryness/

United States Catholic Conference. 2007. *Catechism of the Catholic Church.*
Washington, DC: Libreria Editrice Vaticana.

Meet the authors

Missy Treutel Schmidt

Missy is a Catholic speaker who offers presentations on the power and beautiful fruits of Eucharistic Adoration. Missy and her husband Deacon Ted have been married since 1985 and have five children and six grandchildren... with more on the way.

Kathryn Hayeks White

Kathryn is also available for speaking engagements on Eucharistic Adoration. She and her husband Larry have been married for 47 years and live in beautiful Daphne, Alabama near their three children and four grandchildren.

To contact the authors, visit
www.miraclesonmainst.com

Made in the USA
Columbia, SC
30 April 2024

34766029R00093